THE ART OF

SLOW

READING

Six Time-Honored Practices for Engagement

THE ART OF
S L O W
R E A D I N G

Thomas Newkirk

HEINEMANN
Portsmouth, NH

Heinemann
361 Hanover Street
Portsmouth, NH 03801–3912
www.heinemann.com

Offices and agents throughout the world

The author and publisher wish to thank those who have generously given permission to reprint borrowed material:

Poem entitled "Let Evening Come" by Jane Kenyon from *Collected Poems*. Copyright © 2005 by the Estate of Jane Kenyon. Published by Graywolf Press, Minneapolis, Minnesota. Reprinted by permission of the publisher.

Figure 8–1 from the Bordeaux edition of Michel de Montaigne's essays found on the *Montaigne Studies* website at the University of Chicago, Chicago, Illinois. Reprinted by permission of the University of Chicago.

Library of Congress Cataloging-in-Publication Data
Newkirk, Thomas.
 The art of slow reading : six time-honored practices for engagement / Thomas Newkirk.
  p. cm.
 Includes index.
 ISBN-13: 978-0-325-03731-8
 ISBN-10: 0-325-03731-0
 1. Reading comprehension. I. Title.

LB1050.45.N495 2012
372.47—dc23   2011022820

Editor: *Margaret LaRaia*
Production: *Vicki Kasabian*
Text and cover designs: *Lisa Anne Fowler*
Typesetter: *Kim Arney*
Manufacturing: *Steve Bernier*

Printed in the United States of America on acid-free paper
15 14 13 12   VP   2 3 4 5

CONTENTS

Acknowledgments

This book started in a conversation at the swimming pool. One member of our swimming group, Tom Kelly, is notorious for slowing down a workout—"Hey guys, don't you think we should process this first? Shouldn't we talk about it?" Anyway, between intervals he would talk about the Slow Food Movement and one of its leaders, Carlo Petrini, whom he brought to campus. It got me thinking about the connection between reading and eating—and the role of pleasure in both. It was a start.

I benefited from talks with members at the University of New Hampshire (UNH) community: Sarah Sherman, David Richman, Paula Salvio, Ruth Wharton-McDonald, Janet Schofield, John Lofty, Clark Knowles, and Michael Ferber. Mary Westfall, pastor of the Durham Community Church, was also generous with her time and ideas about reading. And as always, I relied on the consultants in the Learning Through Teaching Program: Ellie Papazaglou, Shirley Smith, Pam Mueller, Penny Kittle, and Jim Webber. I tried out many of the ideas in this book on them—thanks for your patience and good counsel. Louise Wrobleski, Tomasen Carey, Jack Wilde, and Maja Wilson gave me important feedback on an early manuscript draft. I benefited from Emma Carey's reading of the opening chapter at the beginning of the process. My long association with Ellin Keene has been critical in developing the ideas for this book. Special thanks also to Rebecca Webb who has graciously allowed me to draw from her innovative ideas on using mentor texts.

In 2010, I was fortunate to be asked by *Educational Leadership* to write an article on reading (what *were* they thinking?). The wide circulation and extensive response to that piece convinced me that the idea of slow reading resonated for many educators. I was also encouraged by Lori Wright of UNH's media office, which arranged for TV and radio interviews on the topic, as well as for an AP story that was picked up around the country.

Thanks to my department chair, Andy Merton, and my dean, Ken Fuld, who helped me work out a free semester in spring 2011 that allowed me to finish the book ahead of schedule.

Jackie Jorgensen, Mary Ellen Webb, and Liz Wisniewski allowed me into their classrooms, and I am grateful for that opportunity to cite their good work and that of their students. Liz was an encouraging reader of an early draft. Kelly Gallagher also read a full draft and I'm grateful for his response.

I am fortunate and privileged to continue my association with Heinemann, a company I revere. Maura Sullivan was an early supporter of this project. Margaret LaRaia saw it to its conclusion and provided insightful readings. Lisa Fowler once again came up with a knockout cover. Thanks to those involved in the production stage: Vicki Kasabian, Sarah Fournier, Steve Bernier, Cindy Black, Denis Skeean, Michael Loo, and Kim Arney.

On the home front, my wife Beth was a great support, listening to endless rehearsals. My three children have also been great sources of support, and often inspiration (and even material) in my work—remember the drawing of the Happy Puppy Machine, Abby? I also want to express my continued gratitude to my parents, now both deceased, who raised me in a home where reading mattered and where writers held the highest place of honor.

Chapter 1

ABOUT SLOWNESS

What has been is what will be,
what has been done is what will be done;
and there is nothing new under the sun.

ECCLESIASTES 1:9

I am a slow reader. There, it's out.

I can imagine few readers, not even my family members, who will want to read an entire book about my reading process. And this is not such a book. But my own slowness is clearly a motivation for writing. It may take me a week to read a book that, a colleague assures me, I "can read in a night." I've even bookmarked comic books.

I enter a book carefully, trying to get a feel for this writer/narrator/ teller that I will spend time with. I hear the language, feel the movement of sentences, pay attention to punctuation, sense pauses, feel the writer's energy (or lack of it), construct the voice and temperament of the writer. To be sure I visualize, but equally important I auditorize. If I am going to spend time with an author, I want to hear his or her voice—I want some human connection. My spell-checker underlines *auditorize*, so I need to create a rule recognizing it. The fact that there is no recognized word for the phenomenon I want to describe convinces me that there is important work to do here. Because even as I read "silently," I am still in a world of sound. My connection to writers, my pleasure in reading, even my capacity for comprehension depends on this sound, on the voiced quality of print.

I don't hear this voice all the time—when I skim the Internet for facts, or fast-forward through the too-frequent, too-lengthy letters from university administrators. But for reading that truly matters to me, that asks me to be continuously present, I depend on this acoustic connection.

I am thrown off my reading game when I am forced to go too fast. I can feel this connection slipping away. I lose this vital sense of language and rhythm. I am forced to skip, scan, and sample when I feel myself on the clock. As I feel myself pushed beyond a physiological processing limit, one of my favorite and most pleasurable activities becomes suddenly unpleasant. And surely there is no such auditory connection in much of the reading we all do on the Internet where, by some accounts, we "read" about 18 percent of the words on the screen.

But what is *slow reading*? To begin with what it is *not*: It is not the laborious, word-to-word struggle of reading something that is clearly too difficult for a student. Such readers need texts that are easier and more predictable, where they can fluently read for meaning. Nor does *slow reading* mean that there is one ideal speed that everyone should adopt, or even that slowness is always better. Rather, it has to do with the relationship we have with what we read, with the quality of attention that we bring to our reading, with the investment we are willing to make. It is based on the belief that good writing is never consumed, never fully understood, and that although we often read for the efficient extraction of information, this extraction is not the most meaningful or pleasurable reading we do. Slow reading repays even repeated readings and speaks to us in new ways with each reengagement.

To read slowly is to maintain an intimate relationship with a writer. If we are to respond to a writer, we must be *responsible*. We commit ourselves to follow a train of thought, to mentally construct characters, to follow the unfolding of an idea, to hear a text, to attend to language, to question, to visualize scenes. It means paying attention to the decisions a writer makes. Though often characterized as "literary reading," it is relevant to all texts we take seriously. There is usually an ebb and flow to slow reading, periods when we are immersed in the narrative flow, and times when we pause to reflect or reread or just savor the moment. Outside directives that seek to regulate this rhythm (making us stop too often, telling us when to stop, or not giving us the opportunity to stop—even making us go *too* slowly) are profoundly disrupting. Although I am convinced that slow reading is essential for real comprehension, it is also clearly crucial to the deep pleasure we take in reading and for the power of reading to change us. As John Miedema eloquently puts it: "By opening your inner self to a book in this way, you invite ideas and feelings that enrich and expand your interiority. Reading is the making of a deeper self" (65).

. . . even as I read "silently," I am still in a world of sound.

As I have described this writing project to willing and maybe unwilling listeners, I begin to hear their stories. Many of them are slow readers, too. Even English teachers. And like me, many of them claim this slowness to be a real advantage. One extraordinarily talented graduate student admitted that he read silently only a little faster than his oral reading speed. Another admitted to being a subvocalizer. I have come to believe that there is a giant hidden club of slow, proficient readers. I see them in my college classes all the time. They admit they are not "good test-takers" because they think too much about what they read—analogies can go in so many ways. As one student put it, it was so frustrating not to finish the SAT test *that he, after all, had paid to take.* I cannot speak with any authority for this club, but I know it exists.

My own reading story is a very privileged one. My father, a biology professor, was a voracious and eclectic reader, from Montaigne to Mickey Spillane. I would come home from school and I could sometimes hear his voice drifting down from the second floor as he paced and read. He loved Mark Twain and read *The Adventures of Tom Sawyer* to my brother and me several times as a bedtime book. I remember vividly how scary the graveyard scene was. He later bribed us to read both that book and *Huckleberry Finn*—paying us a penny a page. For both of us, there was a ceremonial reading of the last page, and Dad would just shake his head in appreciation of the ending where Huck decides to "light out for new territory" and not go back to the Widow Douglas. "'I been there before,'" my dad would say, quoting Huck, "Isn't that just great? 'I been there before.'"

And from an early age I had contact with writers. My dad loved mosquitoes more than anyone I would ever meet; we grew up with their names as part of our vocabulary (*Culex, Anopheles, Aedes aegypti*), and he would write scientific papers on insects like the dance fly that preyed on mosquitoes. He would send them off to *Annals of the Entomological Society of America*; then, as now, there would be the long wait, and after months he received the decision with the reviewers' comments, which he often resented. I'm convinced I first learned the expression "son of a bitch" in reference to outside reviewers. There would be the two-hour trip to the Ohio State library to incorporate additional citations, the return of the manuscript, and the eventual publication.

His best friend, Dick Snyder, was a poet and short story writer, who brought a steady stream of acclaimed writers to the college campus. We would hear his stories about the literary critic John Crowe Ransom whom he studied with, and of writers like Randall Jarrell, Mary Lavin, Gwendolyn Brooks, or Stephen Spender, all of whom passed through our little town. I once asked Dick's widow, Mary, what she remembered of Ransom, and she said, "Hell of a poker player." In the early '60s, after *Catch-22* became a huge best seller, he had Joseph Heller over to his house. They both flew in bombers during World War II and exchanged war stories. Dick himself talked about his own efforts to place poems, and later let me read drafts of the stories he was working on.

I was privileged to see reading being made by writers, and I could also see the deep affection my father and his friends had for particular writers. Even as a ten-year-old there was no doubt in my mind that James Joyce was more important than Dwight Eisenhower. From an early age, and to this day, reading for me was about an intense relationship with a writer, whose presence I felt. It was reciprocal: the writer was working hard for me (I'd seen it firsthand) and I would work hard as well. I would persist, and together we, the author (or narrator) and I, would enact the story. It was a partnership. Even then, I knew that much of the way I was taught and tested was bogus—texts didn't *have* main ideas, I determined them through my own pattern of attention. Texts didn't have correct interpretations that could be passed on to me. Interpretation was something we did together. Hidden meanings? I didn't believe authors hid things from me, though there was much I discovered in multiple readings. I was loyal to the books and authors I read, and learned to give them my full attention; in fact, reading taught me to be attentive.

This feeling of connection and collaboration was not limited to literary works. I realize that there is no distinction in English education more accepted than the one between literary and nonliterary texts—for example, Louise Rosenblatt's widely cited definitions of *aesthetic* and *efferent reading*. But for me, all good writing is told: In all good writing, even informational texts, I am in the presence of a teller, a narrator, a guide. When things are working, I can sense the writer's engagement, his or her affection for the topic, the delight in the odd fact, the cognitive energy of the piece. I can feel a mind in motion, probing, provoking, defining, anticipating my questions, generating alternatives. It's the kind of writer I try to be—though you can be the judge of that. In fact, as Montaigne noted about his own reading, the gratification comes from attending to the "manner" of the writer's thought process, more than extracting any piece of information.

Although I have titled the book *The Art of Slow Reading*, the ultimate stakes are more important than any literacy issue—it concerns the difficulty we all experience, in this age of distraction, of being *present* in our own lives. To illustrate: A young mother, a teacher in a literacy program in the area, tells the story of her four-year-old talking to her while she is working on her laptop computer. While checking her email, the mother is nodding and acknowledging her daughter, "Yes. Really. Uh-huh." When the daughter comes onto the sofa where her mother is sitting, puts a hand on each of her cheeks, turns her head so they are directly facing each other, and says, "Mommy, I want you to listen with your whole face." But in this age of multitasking, of flitting from website to website (websites designed for viewers to move quickly in and out), these full, sustained acts of attention are often difficult to perform. We are rarely *there*.

Although the Internet and its various applications may make concentration more difficult, the problem of concentration is an old one. In Asian religious traditions, the mind is frequently associated with the monkey, and "monkey mind" refers to the tendency of the mind to be inconstant, capricious, and unsettled. In the Taoist tradition, one of the functions of meditation exercises, like focusing on breathing, is to contain this fluttering tendency, "to lock up the monkey heart." Carl Honore describes the familiar experience of someone trying to focus attention on meditative breathing:

> My mind seemed to have a mind of its own. After five or six breaths, it shoots off like a pinball, ricocheting noisily from one thing to the next. Every time I draw my concentration back to the breath, another barrage of unconnected thoughts comes stampeding through my head—work, family, sports highlights, snippets from pop songs, anything and everything. I begin to worry that there is something wrong with me. (125)

In his classic essay on the shortness of life, in 49 AD Seneca warned against lives that are "busied with many things."

> The space you have, which reason can prolong, although it naturally hurries away, of necessity escapes from you quickly; for you do not seize it, you neither hold it back, nor impose delay upon the swiftest thing in the world, but you allow it to slip away as if it were something superfluous and that could be replaced.

One way to "seize" time is to be open to novelty, to the unexpected, and the possibility of transformation; it is to place a marker in time, to escape, for a moment, the habitual. But novelty requires attention, and when we are rushed, we see what we expect, which is why, I believe, much Internet reading only feeds existing prejudices. In his classic essay, "The Loss of the Creature," Walker Percy points out the difficulty of being truly attentive; even language itself can short-circuit the process. We name something and feel we know it; once it is identified—"Oh, that's a blue heron"—we can go on to other things. Or when we "experience" a major national landmark, the Grand Canyon, for example, we stand at the rim and say, "Wonderful, it looks just like the picture." The thing itself is lost. Of course we still reprimand students and children with "pay attention" as if all we are asking is for mere politeness—when in fact paying attention is one of the hardest things any of us is asked to do.

This is a deeply conservative book, though not in the political sense. In it I try to recuperate older practices of reading—memorization, annotation, meditation, performance—that for millennia helped readers engage deeply and hold onto what they have read. Many of these practices were developed in a time when books were rare and considered precious, and some even sacred. Collections of writing were called *treasuries*. These books could not be consumed, exhausted of meaning, or fully understood. They offered something new with each rereading. I will show how these older practices have relevance today in classrooms—how they can help students, help all of us, perform acts of attention where we are open to particularity, novelty, reflection, to true *experience* in the way that John Dewey used the term. Where we are present in our reading.

The "Pale Hue of Thought"

There's a story about a young school boy in a French school run by an austere and bearded headmaster. One day before the school day began, the boy approached the headmaster, pulled on his sleeve to get his attention, and asked, "Sir, when you sleep do you sleep with your beard above the covers or below the covers?"

The headmaster pushed the boy aside, "Go on, I can't be bothered by such an impertinent question."

But a couple of days later, the headmaster, looking haggard, approached the boy on the playground and shook him angrily. "You little wretch, on account of you I've lost two nights' sleep!"

The moral of the story has to do with the dangers of self-consciousness and the ways it can interfere with the natural and habitual flow of our actions. Hockey goalies warn about the dangers of thinking instead of reacting—and there is an entire literature on "flow" and optimal experience that is free of disruptive self-awareness. In the area of reading, there has been controversy over the use of metacognition, of shifting out of the flow of reading to use comprehension strategies like visualizing and assigning significance. One of the sharpest critics, Nancie Atwell, argues in *The Reading Zone* that, although these strategies have their place in "efferent" reading, they are disruptive in literary reading, particularly the reading of novels where the reader occupies a text world, where he or she is *in* the book. Atwell and others have found students to be resistant to requests to apply sticky notes, to "make connections," to "do strategies," when they are successfully in the flow of the narrative. These requests for metacognitive actions are arbitrary and interfere with the aesthetic experience and pleasure literature can offer.

But a robust approach to engaged reading embraces both the flow of the "reading zone" *and* strategies for reflection. There is a close analogy to Donald Murray's analysis of the writing process in his classic essay, "Teaching the Other Self." Murray claims writing is a dialogue between two versions of the self: a producer and a monitor. One composes, the other looks on, approving, questioning, encouraging, criticizing. I think all writers love the experience of being "in the zone," with the monitor turned off, with words seeming to type themselves, as we "listen to the text." But these runs of language invariably come to an end, and we must shift roles to take on the role of reader and self-prompter. These two roles need to be in creative balance—too powerful a monitor can inhibit our writing; but with no monitor at all, a writer can lose any sense of audience and be unable to reengage with the writing.

The situation is *somewhat* similar in reading. The feeling of being "lost" in a book, of being outside regular time, of being carried forward by our identification with characters and the anticipation of plot, is at the core of our pleasure in reading narratives. And for some books this narrative dream is enough. They don't call upon us to stop or reflect, or deal with difficulty. Many of us became readers by reading such books, and turn to them as adults. Such reading is a mode of pleasure that many students have never experienced—these are the ones who wonder how anyone could sit with a book for so long; the activity puzzles them. Although I am not dealing with this form of immersed reading in this book, I fully acknowledge its importance.

But some books and some reading purposes call on us to be more self-aware—and *this awareness is another mode of pleasure*. Some books pose problems in comprehension—we might feel thrust into a situation that is confusing (*A Tale of Two Cities* is a good example). Unless readers know how to pause and think through these difficulties (and learn that difficulties are natural for many kinds of reading), they will feel inadequate and stupid.

Some texts invite us to attend to the writing itself, to take pleasure in word choices that we may want to linger over. Here is an example from my own current reading, Dickens' *Nicholas Nickelby*. In one scene the sadistic schoolmaster is showing off his son, Wackford Squeers (itself a great name), as a model of how well the boys at his school are fed (a total lie, of course). He pinches his son to show the layers of fat, and tears stream down the poor boy's face, offering even more proof of the boy's well-being:

> "Look at them tears," said Squeers, with a triumphant air, as Master Wackford wiped his eyes with the cuff of his jacket, "there's oiliness." (435)

The choice of *oiliness*, it seems to me, is sheer genius. It perfectly captures the insane connections the headmaster is making, that these tears, this "oil," is the reassuring end product of the diet at Dotheboys Hall. Even copying out this quote makes it more amazing to me. I'd like to think that even Dickens, under extraordinary pressure to meet his deadlines for the serialized book, paused to admire his word choice.

But even for more basic comprehension, readers often need to pause to make sense of what they are experiencing. I recall watching the Zeffirelli version of *Romeo and Juliet*, joined for a while by my six-year-old son who was fooled by the opening scene to think it was an action movie. As the Montagues and Capulets went at it, he asked, "Who are we rooting for?" This was a metacognitive move, a stepping back to fit the play into a schema of good guys/bad guys that he was familiar with. It is the kind of reflective moment that we readers experience as we make our judgment about the characters in books—What do I make of this person? How would I characterize this person? Do I approve or disapprove of his actions? (For the record, I recommended rooting for the Montagues.)

I have good company in this practice, in slowing down to attend to words, as I believe it is a reading practice shared by many writers. Writing is, after all, an act of slow reading; we spend a lot of time with our own sentences; we often shape them slowly, we pause, try to find the right word; we reread them to recapture momentum. One of the first pieces of advice that novelist Francine Prose gives in *Reading Like a Writer* is to slow down and pay attention to words:

> With so much reading ahead of you, the temptation might be to speed up. But in fact it's essential to slow down and read every word. Because one important thing that can be learned by reading slowly is the seemingly obvious but oddly underappreciated fact that language is the medium we use in much the same way that a composer uses notes, the way a painter uses paint. I realize that this may seem obvious, but it's surprising how easily we lose sight of the fact that words are the raw material out of which literature is crafted. (15–16)

Prose, I suspect, would reject the argument that this attention to the medium of literature, to words, interferes with aesthetic pleasure; her point is that this awareness is a form of pleasure. In addition, these moments of awareness, the pause to appreciate a word choice like *oiliness*, teaches readers the craft of writing.

A key factor in all this is that I am choosing; I am following my own pattern of connections, significance. I lose myself in plot as I choose to, and stand back to reflect when I choose to. No one is regulating for me this pattern of attention. There are no questions at the end of the book, and I would ignore them if there were. No one is telling me when to stop and reflect or what to reflect about. No one is rewarding me for the number of stops I make. This reading is a private affair between me and the writer, Charles Dickens, with whom I have had a long relationship. It began when I was twelve and attended an auction in town where I bid twenty-five cents for his collected works, an oversized six-volume set, too big for me to carry the mile or so to my house. Later that day I hauled them home in my red wagon.

I suspect that many who glorify the technological changes that surround us, who revel in the multiple stimuli that beg for our attention, will find this opening one more sad, nostalgic lament for an earlier age that may not have even existed except for a handful of readers. They will say that my advocacy of slowness and deliberateness (and books that ask this of us) is a doomed appeal for a highly inefficient form of reading. That my advocacy for slowness is precisely the wrong advice for an age when students need the processing speed to handle so much information. They will say it is doomed because these new technologies create new forms of intelligence; they rewire our brains in new ways, with losses and gains—too bad if no one wants to (or can) read *Nicholas Nickelby*, all eight hundred pages. Steven Johnson, the author of *Everything Bad Is Good for You*, claims that the new technologies don't eliminate reading, they make it more connected and social—for a small loss in the ability to focus, we get almost unimaginable connection and access:

> The speed with which we can follow the trail of an idea, or discover new perspectives on a problem, has increased by several orders of magnitude. We are marginally less focused and exponentially more connected. That's a bargain all of us should be happy to make. ("Yes, People," BU 3)

Johnson may be right—though I wouldn't bet on it. It seems to me a casual and myopic dismissal of powerful traditional forms of reading—and it fails to appreciate the human need for depth and reflection.

"What Has Been Will Be Again"

I have subtitled this book *Six Time-Honored Practices for Engagement*. In doing so, I have avoided the ubiquitous "research-based" claim. I don't mean to suggest that current research on comprehension is, in any way, at odds with what I propose. Good readers are active and strategic—they pose questions, build predictions, visualize, infer, and fit what they read into wider patterns. They monitor their reading: in effect, they can watch themselves determine when something doesn't make sense or when they have lost the drift of what they have read. They pay attention. They benefit from the demonstrations of skilled readers. And good readers *read a lot*—there is an undeniable correlation between reading practice and reading skill (it would be hard to imagine the opposite case). It follows *"paying attention" is one of the hardest things any of us is asked to do.*

that good readers take some pleasure in reading; it is functional for them, and not merely some task performed for others. I cannot expect much disagreement from any serious empirical reading researcher on any of these practices.

The weakness, the profound weakness, of much educational research and in-school testing is evasion on the question of values. The root of evaluation is, obviously, the term *value*—and the premise of assessment must be that it tests something that we as a culture value. But in most research, this logic gets turned on its head—and the assessment instrument *becomes* the value. We all want our students to do well on tests, but how many of us know what values underlie these tests? What principles of reading do they stress? Ignore? I suspect few teachers or even reading specialists could answer this question, yet we (and those who evaluate us) are reassured when students do well on them. The technical term for this kind of assurance is *reification*—giving solidity (making it a thing, *res* in Latin) to something that is really a construct or an idea or proposition. Comprehension becomes identical to doing well on this test; the test, rather than being built on a value system, becomes the value system. We become our numbers.

Those who raise questions about the validity of standardized tests are often perceived as hopelessly unscientific and impractical. *But*, the very logic of testing, and of validity (which also has *value* as its root), necessitates this questioning. We must ask what reading is. What's it for? What function should or can it have in our lives? If, for example, we claim that one of the values we profess is that students develop the habit of reading (as I do), we have to look at *that*; we have to assess *that*. If we believe that speed is a fundamentally important trait of good readers (as I don't), we can set tight time limits. If we believe that texts have determinate and fixed meanings arrived at reliably through inferences (as I don't), we can assess comprehension through right-or-wrong multiple-choice questions. If we believe that reading is part of an activity system, usually multimodal, where it is *used* in some way (as I do), it needs to be assessed within these complex systems. This is not an antiscientific bias against assessment; it is the essence, the core justification, of assessment—the *value* in evaluation.

We have many important ways of knowing, many sources of wisdom. Comparative research studies comprise a part of that knowledge but only a part; they can, at their best, let us know about tendencies in large populations. Teachers, on the other hand, work in individual and fluid situations that change by the minute. The same child may respond differently at different times of the day; he may have a different style of learning than his sister. Activities that work well for one teacher feel alien to another. Consequently, the fine-grained observational and decision-making skills and self-knowledge of the teacher are profoundly important. This "gold standard" comparative research rarely provides the certainty, or the situational specificity, that teachers need. And even the history of medical research, the model for much current educational research, is littered with research findings that have been overturned (anyone recall hormone replacement therapy?).

Reading and writing are cultural practices, not just technical proficiencies. They are embedded in rituals, cultures, institutions, and histories—all of which provide us with another important kind of knowledge. We learn to read and write in order to participate in cultures and communities, to connect with others, to enter the mysteries of religious experience, to do the work of the world, to share responses to literature, and to sometimes literally pledge allegiance to institutions. They are value laden. Many of these practices have long histories that are usually ignored in educational research when references rarely reach back more than twenty years. History has weight and authority, and the traditions of literacy practice, over centuries, should not be dismissed—or, if so, it will be our loss. Their very persistence gives them credibility. We can fantasize that we are in a new information age that makes all that came before outdated, that our brains are being wired differently, that our brains move faster. That in having access to so much more information, we have transcended limitations of previous generations. But I suspect we only fool ourselves when we do.

A few years ago, I visited Hadrian's Wall in northern England. Crossing the entire width of England, it was built around 122 AD to mark the limits of the Roman Empire. Various Roman forts were built along the wall, and near one of them was a museum that reconstructed life there 1,900 years ago. The exhibit that shocked me was one that had to do with footwear; apparently dozens of discarded shoes and sandals were buried in a pit that preserved them perfectly. As I looked at this tangle, I could pick out a near-exact model of the Teva sandals I wore; there were leather versions of flip-flops, and just about every other variation. This tangle of preserved footwear was a cautionary example, a reminder of the expertise and ingenuity of those who lived long before our time. There are, to be sure, many forward-looking books, written in the confidence that we have transcended our own history, that we have advanced so far and so fast, that it is no longer relevant—that it's safe to be ahistorical. That we can know where we are going without knowing where we came from. Clearly I find this view myopic and arrogant.

I presumptuously hope that this will be a book relevant to literacy teachers at all grade levels. There are, obviously, issues specific to different age groups and competency levels; the second grader is different from the first grader (one of my colleagues called second grade "the adolescence of elementary school"). But there are practices and issues we all have in common. I myself have learned so much about teaching from watching primary school teachers. Good ideas, sound practices, I am convinced work at all levels—though it calls upon the ingenuity of teachers to adapt them.

I recently watched a wonderful video, developed in New Zealand, that presented four student cases in a Reading Recovery program—all struggling readers, about as far from my own students in age and reading level as I could imagine. At first, almost all of these readers would "read" without attending to the words—from memory, from picture cues (one student "read" by recalling the wrong book). A real early milestone in each case occurred when the student would voluntarily reread, when they would recognize that the word they read didn't make sense, or didn't match the letters, or maybe they just weren't sure of it. These moments, strongly praised by the great teachers in the video, distill the essence of thinking at all age levels: recognizing a difficulty and employing a strategy to deal with it, then retesting to see if that revision worked better. Whatever our teaching level, we can all learn from these demonstrations of excellent teaching.

In many ways, this will be a backward-looking book, though I hope a practical one. It will be appreciative of tradition and cultural practice. This does not mean that I minimize teacher initiative and decision making or that I dislike the new technologies that I am using at this very instant—because every situation we face as teachers is new in some way.

But to live in traditions is to have roots. It means we are not swayed by the wind of each passing trend; that although attention to research is important, we are not subservient to it; that we are properly skeptical of expert opinion (which historically has often been wrong and often in the service of commercial interests). To live in traditions is to have allies and heroes—John Dewey, Mike Rose, Robert Frost, Louise Rosenblatt, Peter Elbow, Peter Johnston, Erasmus, St. Augustine, Donald Murray, Michel de Montaigne—a galaxy of great thinkers who have made a compelling case for literacy and learning at its most engaging.

I'll make my stand with them.

Chapter 2

THE SPEED CURRICULUM

Speed her up, 401.

—THE PRESIDENT OF ELECTRO STEEL IN
CHARLIE CHAPLIN'S *MODERN TIMES*

*The faster one goes, the more strain there is on the
senses, the more they fail to take in, the more confusion
they must tolerate or gloss over—and the longer it takes
to bring the mind to a stop in the presence of anything.*

WENDELL BERRY, "AN ENTRANCE TO THE WOODS"

Charlie Chaplin's classic film *Modern Times* opens with an image of a clock. The scene then shifts to the Electro Steel Company, where Chaplin's character works on an assembly line tightening an endless succession of nuts on metal plates (we never learn what is actually being made). Time and efficiency are paramount. Just before lunch, the company president meets representatives from the Billows Feeding Machine, who want to demonstrate their invention that will keep the lunch break from being a drain on productivity.

They choose Chaplin as a "volunteer," and he is locked, standing, into the device, his arms immobilized while a tray rotates at face level. He is forcibly fed from this rotating tray. Mechanical arms push meat cubes into his mouth, an ear of corn is placed in his mouth and rotated, a sponge-like face wiper swings in and cleans his lips. Within seconds the machine develops a short, sparks fly, and the action gets diabolically fast. The corn rotates wildly, kernels fly until Chaplin momentarily stops the spinning with his nose; soup is dumped down his front; the mechanical wiper repeatedly smacks him in the face. At one point, the Billows technician carelessly places loose nuts from the malfunctioning machine on the tray, and these are pushed into Chaplin's mouth. It is a scene that is both wildly funny and terrifying; our laughter is uneasy, he seems so vulnerable (one imagines it must have been a dangerous scene to shoot). At the end of the demonstration, the Electro Steel President says he is not interested. "It's not efficient."

I like to show this scene to teachers and ask them to write for a few minutes to explore any parallels to their school situations. They don't get far into the writing—they want to talk. They recognize what Raymond Callahan calls this "cult of efficiency": the overloading of the curriculum where things are added but nothing subtracted; the way that their work is increasingly managed by others; images of speed like Arne Duncan's "Race to the Top" or the popular reading program Accelerated Reader; the indigestible mix of programs that clutter and contend in their schools, making the day increasingly hectic; the focus on measurement and speed; the push for performance and pacing.

Some mention methods of assessing young children's reading of nonsense syllables where the teacher literally holds a stopwatch. Years ago the term *hidden curriculum* was used to describe a set of unacknowledged values that schools promoted. The child on the stopwatch must surely learn that schools reward speed (though we might call it "fluency"), that it is the primary virtue, the basic quality of a good reader, a good student. That it's a race. This value system will be reinforced again and again as students take tests—invariably timed—throughout their school careers.

Current definitions of *fluency* sensibly combine "expression" and reading rate, yet when it comes to calculating fluency, expression often drops out of the picture. Expression is, after all, so subjective. Established formulae determine fluency by words per minute minus reading errors; the faster, the more fluent. It is a measure of productivity, efficiency, output. One question that will surely be raised about "slow reading" is how it relates to research on fluency. Good readers process text through a series of *saccades*, or jumps in which the eye and brain take in groups of words. This recognition of words is automatic, enabling cognitive effort to concentrate on higher functions of comprehension. By contrast, weaker readers are often plodders, stopped frequently by unfamiliar words ("big words" become frightening). Struggling readers often seem to scan ahead for big words, which act like land mines in their reading. They flinch and lose concentration, regress, backtrack—and in the process spend so much time in mere decoding, they lose track of meaning. Clearly the "slow reading" being advocated in this book is not this halting, inefficient, often intimidated reading process.

...fluency can never be a race.

There is a danger, however, is associating fluency too closely with speed. The widely used DIBELS assessment requires regular short tests of all students, which create a measure of "nonsense word fluency." When I first heard this term, it seemed an oxymoron—*fluency*, as I had come to understand it, was the effective and meaningful processing of real, connected, communicative language. Questions are read as questions. Dialogue is read with appropriate expression. Punctuation acts as a significant indicator of meaning. The reader has caught the voice of the text and the intent of the author. *Fluency* in this sense is indivisible from *comprehension*—a fluent reader demonstrates comprehension.

And fluency can never be a race. Faster is not always better. In fact, a reader who reads too fast—running over periods and pauses (or skipping words altogether in a skimming fashion)—would not be reading fluently, as I would define it. A fluent reader takes his cues from the text. In a recent review of research, Timothy Rasinski and Pamela Hamman note that current instructional practices, motivated by federal policy, are pushing students to read faster (and indeed the norms for reading speed have gone up), but these increases in speed have not been matched by improvement in comprehension. Reading fluency has become, in their words, "a speed-reading contest." We should go in the opposite direction, they argue:

> The importance of speed should be minimized in the fluency debate. Reading requires a level of active awareness and thought about language which diminishes when reading speed is emphasized. Reading at the appropriate rate in meaningful phrases, with prosody and comprehension, should be the fluency goal for all readers. The literate person is one who derives meaning, not speed, from the printed word. (2010, 26)

One might also add that the literate person derives pleasure from finding this appropriate tempo of reading.

Recently I interviewed an admired theatre teacher at the University of New Hampshire to ask him about his reading process. David Richman has been blind from birth and for most of his life has read Braille, which he claims cannot be skimmed. His silent reading speed is the same as his oral reading speed:

> Reading has always been for me a sensuous experience. I love to read aloud. I love to get my mouth around the words. And even if I am not reading aloud, I am the kind of person that Mary McCarthy wrote about in the famous essay disparaging people who move their lips as they read. I am one of those readers. I read slowly, and it has always been an enormous advantage for me because it has allowed me to retain what I read—and when you get into this business (the theatre), you have to have a retentive memory. (Personal interview, July 6, 2010)

I am not claiming that David Richman's reading process should be the norm (though it resembles mine), only that he is clearly a fluent reader, and he would not be a more fluent reader if he went faster. Fluency is an attunement to the text, an act of attentiveness, an alertness to mood, voice, punctuation—even to what he calls the "sensuousness" of language. A reader can be wonderfully fluent reading at the pace of oral reading, as Richman does. By attaching the term *fluency* to the timed tests like those of DIBELS, the program inappropriately claims a value beyond sheer speed of processing; it conflates sense and nonsense. One might even argue that the word *word* is also co-opted—is a "nonsense word" in fact a "word"? The only word that survives scrutiny in "nonsense word fluency" is *nonsense*.

I believe it also tells a dangerous story about reading and learning to young children—that speed is key, that reading is a race, that the stopwatch rules. In a published letter to Michelle Obama, one seven-year-old promised that in third grade she would learn how to take tests better: She would try to learn faster and practice the test much faster. That was her wish. But what sort of classroom instruction leads to a goal like this one ("Dear First Lady")?

Fluency can mean slowing down as well. Take this opening passage from Jack Gantos' memoir, *Hole in My Life*:

> The prisoner in the photograph is me. The ID number is mine.
> The photo was taken in 1972 in a medium-security Federal
> Correctional Institution in Ashland, Kentucky. I had been
> locked up for a year already—the bleakest year of my life—and I
> had more time ahead of me. (3)

To be sure, this passage provides us with key information for the book, but it does much more. If it were scored for music, the tempo would be adagio, slow, a lament. Gantos, bit by painful bit, is making a series of admissions, almost as if there were a sigh at the end of the first two sentences. We get a mood of deep regret—if we allow ourselves to take it in. If we don't rush. Paradoxically, I would argue that a quick, glancelike reading of this opening is *not* a mark of fluency because it would disregard the tempo of the text.

Even for basic comprehension, we often have to slow down and imagine a text as performed; we might be able to read all the words, but miss the purpose or action of those words. Take, for example, two lines spoken by Richard II in Act IV, Scene 1 of the play, at the critical moment when the unstable king is asked if he is "contented" to give up his crown:

> Ay, no; no, ay; for I must nothing be;
> Therefore no, no, for I resign to thee.

I suspect the "reading level" for this passage would be quite low—but what a task for understanding! How are we to imagine this sequence of *ays* and *noes*? Is the first *Ay*, ironic—like he's saying, "What a stupid question?" How is his mind flitting around? How is he disagreeing with himself? Are the *noes* in the second line softer, more "resigned," than those in the first? What do we make of the *Therefore*—implying a logical move; but what is the logic? The sequence becomes more interesting the more we look at it—and if we are to understand it, we need to imagine it performed if only in our head.

In his introduction to an issue of *Ploughshares*, the editor Charles Baxter makes a similar point. He notes that he chose stories that stopped him, transfixed him at moments, played to his "weakness for stillness and wonder." And he ends his introduction with this advice to readers:

> For your own good, your skills of efficient speed reading—if you have them—might well be, as we now say, disengaged. Some pleasures, usually the best ones, take their own sweet time, and although literature has no traffic cops, if it did, and I were one such cop, I would be stopping the graduates of the Evelyn Wood Institutes to ask, "Hey. What's your hurry?" What is profound or psychically consequential often allows its pivotal elements a kind of suspension in the midst of an onward narrative flow, and each one of these stories has the power to suspend itself, like a trapeze artist who flies into the air and somehow, despite the forces of gravity (and of time) manages to stay transfixed, by us, above the net. (Introduction)

Yet this is hardly the image of reading that schools—or consequential tests—present to students.

One of my college freshmen, Evan Nadeau, wrote an essay about what he felt was the unfairness of time being such a factor in evaluating reading on the SAT test. Here is his description on taking the test:

> When the time began and I opened the first page, I noticed that the first section was reading comprehension. There was a two-page single-spaced excerpt followed by about thirty multiple-choice questions requiring in-depth analysis of the reading. I was shocked. I am unfortunately a slow reader, and I knew

that if I took time to actually read the full excerpt, I would have only been left with about five to ten minutes to answer as many questions as I could. I looked around to the other students taking the exam, and I noticed some were already answering questions and others were reading vigorously. I could feel myself getting overwhelmed, getting flushed, worried and sweating, and I began to skim through the reading as fast as I could and answer the questions.

I had never experienced time to elapse so quickly as it did during that test. By the time the man in the front of the room said, "Pencils down! Close your question booklets," I had only finished fifteen questions. I was upset, with reason. The test seemed tailored for students who could read fast, and finish fast, not for the average slow test-taker like myself. Also, I was paying a lot of money for a test that did not allow me to complete it in its entirety. As I looked around, I could see others feeling the same way I felt, and some looking confident and happy about how they did. I was jealous.

Unnerved by this section of the test, he had time difficulty with other parts, receiving a score of 1250 out of 2400, putting this obviously competent student in the lower 30th percentile in the country. The test, he claimed, undermined one of his most significant qualities as a student: "I like to take my time, concentrate and make sure that the answers I am giving are my absolute final decision." Evan has good company in this complaint. The noted educator and cognitive researcher Howard Gardner has argued for the elimination of these time constraints:

> Few tasks in life—and very few tasks in scholarship—actually depend on the ability to read passages or solve math problems rapidly. . . . Indeed by eliminating the timed component the College Board would signal that background knowledge, seriousness of purpose, and effort—not speed and glibness—are the essentials of good scholarship. And if, in the future, students are allowed to use dictionaries, or even to access the Web, so much the better. Such a change will far more accurately duplicate the conditions under which serious individuals at any level of expertise actually do their work.

Of course, removing these constraints would make the logistics of test administration extraordinarily difficult (and increase the cost)—so the College Board is likely to strenuously fight for these limits.

There are other reasons for a strong time limitation. Anyone who has taken the SAT verbal tests—or any standardized test for that matter—has felt this time pressure. We have become used to it. It seems as normal as the #2 pencil and the scripted directions from the teacher administering the test. Yet the testing situation creates errors of profoundly different types. The SAT test conflates these two kinds of errors—those caused by an inability to comprehend and those caused by haste. Both count equally against the student. Why should a test of comprehension have anything to do with speed?

But if we were to do a thought experiment, the logic of the SAT emphasis on speed would be evident. To create an effective test, the designers at the College Board and the ACT (where the time pressures are more severe) *must induce errors*—enough to create a healthy spread of scores. Let's say, to be perverse, that on the reading comprehension part of this test, students were given as much time as they wanted so that the persistent slow readers, like Evan, could check their answers, reread passages if necessary. And let's say that this opportunity meant that fewer errors were made by all students—it would be hard to find passages and questions so hard that Evan couldn't crack them, given time. The bell curve would be compressed because errors forced by speed and failure to complete the test would be minimized. With fewer errors made, scores would be more unstable—missing one or two more items might drop a score substantially. *In short, a test like the SAT depends on errors induced by speed.*

Evan's description of taking the SAT test illustrates how disruptive it can be to be thrown off a natural activity pace (athletes continually talk about "finding a rhythm"). There is a clear analogy to finding one natural speed in hiking. Each summer I take a group of teachers to the White Mountains. For many, it is their first experience with mountain hiking; they have never climbed the old stream beds and stone ledges of this great trail system. One thing I stress is to find a natural pace for climbing—nothing is more stressful and unpleasant than having to hike at a pace faster than one's natural pace. They need to find a level of exertion that doesn't leave them constantly winded or where they feel their energy draining from them and their legs getting so heavy that they must force themselves forward. They need to know their own bodies and to allow themselves to pause and rest in the steeper sections; to feel comfortable with their balance as they move from rock to rock. It is not a race. A good hiker is not a fast hiker, but one who can find this natural pace. "Take your time," I say. "If some people finish early, we can wait." This natural pace gets quicker, our balance more assured with practice, but there is a huge variation in this natural pace—just as I see among my students with reading. It is seriously disruptive and uncomfortable to be forced to accelerate this natural pace; it often means suspending reading altogether and sampling a text, reading first sentences, beginnings and endings, things we would never choose to do on our own.

Carlo Petrini, one of the forces in the Slow Food movement, calls this natural pace the "tempo guisto." He is not advocating—and I am not advocating—that everything needs to be done slowly, or that we are more virtuous or more effective if we uniformly slow down. "Being Slow," he explains, "means that you control the rhythms of your own life. You decide how fast you have to go in any given context. If today I want to go fast, I go fast; if tomorrow I want to go slow, I go slow. What we are fighting for is the right to determine our own tempos" (quoted in Honore, 16). The implications for reading are, I believe, enormous, because specialists routinely specify a normative speed, and those for whom this is an unnatural tempo feel inadequate. *Slow*, after all, has long been a euphemism for *stupid*.

Since raising this issue of slowness in an article in *Educational Leadership*, I have received a number of emails from readers who have felt some stigma for their own slowness, like this one from a Native American radio producer, working in Alaska, who had heard a radio show on which some students from our summer writing academy participated:

> I am a slow reader and have never been able to read fast. Over the years I took classes to help me read faster but to no avail. Finally I resigned myself to the fact that I would never be a fast reader but learned to treasure that I took in more information

or understood better than people who read faster. It used to embarrass me that a book many people could read in a day or two would take me a week to read. . . .

I love reading and I never let my slowness drive me away from reading. I read at the pace it takes to read out loud and so I have found it very enjoyable to listen to audiobooks. . . . After listening to the radio story about the Writers Academy and slow reading, I realized that my slow reading may have helped me become the good writer I am today. I never thought of it in that way. So I want to say "Thank you" for helping me realize that maybe slow reading isn't a handicap after all.

Here is a reader with a process that he finds both pleasurable and effective—yet for years he lived with the belief that his slowness was a handicap. What kind of educational system creates this stigma?

As a slow reader myself, I can recall that clammy feeling that came when I anticipated the longer and harder passages near the end of the test, and I would have to resort to reading practices I never used elsewhere. But my moment of true intimidation came in college. In my sophomore year at Oberlin College, Alan Pearl, an upperclassman and history major, bragged that he could read one thousand pages in a day. The rest of us took up the bet, though there was some negotiating about the terms: what kind of reading (no novels, it had to be reading for his major), what kind of assessment (no picky questions about facts, but more general themes). Once these were agreed upon, we chose a day, cleared the lounge where Alan sat in a thronelike armchair, books at his side, and we would occasionally look in for an update and page count. As I recall, it was a weekday, but in 1968, we had begun to take class schedules as *suggestions*.

Around 7:00, he announced he was done, and the inquest began, with David Gottlieb the primary questioner. Bismarck's social reforms. British naval policy. The turmoil in France during 1848. Frederick the Great and Voltaire. Pearl had it all. Occasionally, Gottlieb gave him part credit, but after thirty minutes, the verdict was clear. Pearl was victorious. He and several floor mates went off to drink (or maybe smoke) in celebration, while I just sat there in awe. I rarely read a tenth of that amount in a day—and that effort often left me exhausted. Pearl's performance left me feeling completely overmatched and uncertain about any academic career that involved extensive reading.

The Clock in the Mind

It's worthwhile to reflect on that opening image that Chaplin gives us—the clock. Our sense of time is not somehow "natural"—it results from an internalization of structures (seconds, minutes) produced by clocks. When clocks came into use in the fourteenth century, this technology began to change human consciousness. Punctuality became a virtue—to be as "regular as clockwork." According to Lewis Mumford, Westerners quickly became so thoroughly conditioned to clock time that it became "second nature," indeed a fact of nature and not a human invention. Clocks created the idea of time as quantifiable units; they created the sense of "moment to moment." According to Neil Postman, "The clock has the effect of disassociating time from human events and thus nourishes the belief in an independent world of mathematically measured sequences" (11). This invention was critical for the coordination and mechanical efficiency of industrial development and complex social organizations, but it undercut what philosopher Henri Bergson called "duration," in which a time sense came from a more organic and biological attunement to activity and nature, where eating times might be dictated by hunger and not the clock, where days have different length depending on the availability of sunlight.

In this state of complete involvement, we escape "the tyranny of time."

This clock consciousness can bring about a form of alienation. We are often in two places at the same time—as any teacher knows. We are attending to what students are saying, doing, hopefully learning, but we are also attending to the clock in our heads. (Is it time to move on? Will I have time for free reading? Why is the Special late in getting here?) At times, we may let these considerations keep us from being effective listeners or observers because we are not fully present in our own classrooms. Studies of teacher wait time dramatically demonstrate our acute sensitivity to the passage of time.

At the same time, I expect we long to escape this double consciousness, to slip the awareness of the clock, of units of time. "Where has the time gone?" we ask when we are deeply engaged and emerge into a more clock-conscious state of mind. Sven Birkerts describes a "reading state" in which time is felt in a special way:

> In this state, when all is clear and right, I feel a connectedness that cannot be duplicated (unless, maybe, when the act of writing is going well). I feel an inside limberness, a sense of being for once in accord with time—real time, deep time. Duration time, within which events resonate and *mean*. When I am at my finest pitch of reading, I feel as if my life—past as well as unknown future—were somehow available to me. (83–84)

Birkerts does not define what he means by "duration time," but I take that to mean a state of mind when we are completely attuned to what we are doing; passage of time is felt in terms of the activity itself and not externally existing clock time (which he would say is not "real time"). In this state of complete involvement, we escape "the tyranny of time" (67).

There was a dramatic, and politically significant, demonstration of these different forms of time in one of the 1992 presidential debates between Bill Clinton and George Herbert Bush. Near the end of the debate, as Clinton was speaking, Bush looked at his watch as if to see how much longer it would go on—that was all. We need something like the concept of "duration time" to understand the offense that many viewers felt at Bush's action, the way it damaged his ethos at that moment. As potential voters, we want politicians in this situation to be so engaged in presenting their ideas, so into "duration time," that they don't even think about when the debate would be over (even as we expect them to respect time limits for responses). Whether they actually feel this way, they have to *appear to*. Bush's glance at his watch seemed to betray a time consciousness that viewers interpreted as a lack of full engagement with the debate.

In *Modern Times*, after the eating machine demonstration, Chaplin returns to the assembly line, twisting the nuts on the metal plates. The president of the company orders the line to go to full speed, and Chaplin turns manic, lying on the assembly line, tightening, tightening until he is taken into the big gears of the machine—one of the iconic images in American cinema. It is the ultimate chaos. He has gone crazy, become the machine, the assembly line must be (momentarily) stopped and reversed to extract him. Mary Ann Reilly, in her essay "Dressing the Corpse: Professional Development and the Play of Singularities," describes a situation in a contemporary, program-driven reading classroom that is an exact analogy to Chaplin's factory.

Reilly describes a second-grade reading lesson taught by a beginning teacher whom she calls Ms. Sheridan, who teaches in an urban school with 84 percent of students qualifying for free lunches. Prompted by requirements in the Reading First Program, the district has adopted the Harcourt Trophies core reading program and has set up pacing charts and an assessment schedule for implementation. Ms. Sheridan is expected to complete all thirty-six of the basal units by the end of the school year. In the lesson Reilly describes, Ms. Sheridan is having students read chorally George Ancona's *Helping Out*, a photo essay on—ironically, it turns out—cooperation between children and adults. She begins the lesson, with the teacher's guide in the crook of her arm; she looks up and says, "Get ready." But students are not ready—some don't have their books open, and one student has the wrong book. After six minutes and several "Get ready" prompts, students begin their reading. Here is Reilly's description of the choral reading:

> Ms. Sheridan and the children read the name of the title and
> the author aloud and then continue on to the essay. As there
> are different reading rates, the choral quality is poor. Even
> with the text in front of me, I find it challenging to follow as
> the loudness of the reading increases and the voices become
> more disjointed.
>
> I am startled when Ms. Sheridan gets to the bottom of the
> first page and yells, "turn," and the children, regardless of where
> they are in the text, turn the page and continue reading. This
> process of reading loudly, punctuated by Ms. Sheridan occa-

sionally saying "turn," continues for several more pages. Lost in the process are phrasing, tone, and meaning. Given the reading pace, there is also no time to actually view the photographs. As the loudness seems to increase, I am relieved to see the end of the essay at hand. Yet when Ms. Sheridan arrives at the bottom of what I think is the last page, she tells the children to turn the page. Like the children I turn the page and see the essay has ended and now there is a poem. I am surprised that Ms. Sheridan and her students continue reading aloud. There is no pause between the essay and poem.

The choral reading is followed by a series of questions on the main idea of the selection in which she finally gets the answer she wants, "Helping out," and reminds students to look to the title for help with the main idea.

After the lesson, Reilly interviewed Ms. Sheridan about her decision to read the selection chorally:

> "You do 10 pages a day if you're going to finish the program," she says pointing to the pacing chart. "Ten pages every day from the basal, workbooks, or little books. There's a lot there. It's just hard to do it all. I have to test their fluency and so the reading out loud helps children get faster. They need to read so *many* words in a minute . . . Some can't even read 10. So we practice reading fast. There's a lot to get in each week and you got to keep the pace going." (88–90)

This teacher is just as much on the assembly line as Chaplin. Decisions about content and pacing are taken away from her (even though, paradoxically, she is given regular assessment data that her scripted curriculum precludes her from using). Her work is "alienated labor" in the Marxian sense. It bears no relationship to her individuality as a human being. The not-so-hidden curriculum is *speed*; it is paramount in her consciousness, central to her experience of accountability, and an element of the curriculum she has no control over. Reilly concludes her account, "When I think of Ms. Sheridan and her students, I think of potential being denied" (92).

My point, and Reilly's as well, is not to callously criticize a beginning teacher for making mistakes; mistakes go with the territory and are essential for reflective thought. But on this assembly line, there is no opportunity (or right) to question the pacing guides, to argue that students need more time. The pace of instruction becomes a fact of nature, as inevitable as the sunrise. She is caught in the machine.

Even when we are not on the clock like Ms. Sheridan, it is so easy to rush ourselves, and the proliferation of educational goals and expectations is a big part of the problem. The standards movement has, in my view, failed in its primary mission—to *focus*, to direct attention to essentials, to concentrate effort. Curriculum, after all, is about saying "No." There are infinite skills that could be mastered, facts to be learned, theories to be explored. It is hard to argue against any of them. But teaching requires the discipline to say "Yes" to a few of these, and "No" to most of them. Otherwise, our efforts are scattered and superficial. Unfortunately, tragically, that discipline is sorely lacking in many of the standards documents. Take, for example, one standard from the tenth-grade California history standards:

> Compare and contrast the Glorious Revolution of England, the American Revolution, and the French Revolution and their enduring effects worldwide on the political expectations for self-government and individual liberty. (In Gallagher, 38)

As Kelly Gallagher notes, teachers could easily spend a year on this objective, for example, extending to the breakup of the Soviet Union, the collapse of British Imperialism, the Civil Rights Movement. *But, this is only one of forty-nine standards for tenth grade.* Texts for AP Biology can include as many as 56 chapters and 1,400 pages—all of it testable, leading to what some teachers call "an organ a day" instruction—a situation the College Board has committed to change (Drew).

As a teacher in college, I can't blame testing or the standards movement for my teaching mistakes—which are invariably ones of haste and impatience. I rarely make teaching mistakes because I am too deliberate; it is always the other way around. I leave out steps, plunge into an activity too quickly, fail to illustrate what I mean, assume that by naming a process I have explained it.

And then I'm surprised.

My students come into class with their reading assignments completely unmarked, pages as pristine as the day the book came out of the wrapper. I initially interpret this as a casual approach to my assignment, that is, until I realize that I had not bothered to ask them to mark the book, or that I failed to realize that in high school they could get in trouble for marking a book, or to explain that the used-book market was such a rip-off they shouldn't worry about marking, or to show them ways of marking a book. I was a victim of what Mike Rose calls "assumptive teaching"; I had failed to decenter, to imagine *their* procedural knowledge, to be explicit. So as I work with teachers, I push them to be deliberate, to slow down and think through the kind of explicit instructions they might give, to think through front-loading activities that need to precede the work they want students to do. In the animal fables, slowness triumphs. So my motto for them is "The turtle always wins." Always.

The Culture of Distraction

> Yet the time which they enjoy is short and swift, and it is made
> that much shorter by their own fault; for they flee from one
> pleasure to another and cannot remain fixed in one desire.
> —Seneca, "On the Shortness of Life"

Neil Postman provides a foundation for my argument in his classic, *Teaching as a Conserving Activity*. Schools, Postman argues, should act on a thermostatic principle: a thermostat acts to cool when a room is too hot, to heat when too cool. Schools should act to check (and not imitate) some tendencies in the wider information environment: "The major role of education in the years immediately ahead is to help conserve that which is necessary to a humane survival and threatened by a furious and exhausting culture" (25). It follows that schools need to take a stand for an alternative to an increasingly hectic digital environment where reading and writing are done in severely abbreviated messages and clicks of the mouse.

The same case might be made for church services that conceivably could make more use of technology—surely we could follow a sermon better if the key points were projected on PowerPoint that we could later download. Yet innovations like this would likely be viewed by many traditionalists as unwelcome intrusions into a space where a different form of attention is expected. The regularity and predictability and pace of worship are deeply reassuring. They stand against the volatility of the media environment in the wider culture. In Postman's terms, the church fills a *conserving* role, a thermostatic counterweight to what goes on outside. Many parents have this same sense about schools, appreciating the regularities of grades, proms, homework, and classroom organizations of orderly desks. They quietly mourn the decline of penmanship and grammar instruction (even if they disliked it when they were students).

Postman's work appeared before the arrival of the Internet (his major target was television). But it assumes new relevancy in the current information environment where so much is so instantly available—leading to concerns for the future of reading itself. Nicholas Carr's controversial essay "Is Google Making Us Stupid?" makes the case that the Internet undermines traditional forms of attentive and sustained reading:

> Over the past few years I've had an uncomfortable sense that someone, or something, has been tinkering with my brain. . . . My mind isn't going—so far as I can tell—but it's changing. I'm not thinking the way I used to think. I can feel it most strongly when I am reading. Immersing myself in a book or lengthy article used to be easy. My mind would get caught up in the narrative or turns of the argument, and I'd spend hours strolling through long stretches of prose. Now my concentration starts to drift after two or three pages. I get fidgety, lose the thread, begin looking for something else to do. I feel as if I am always dragging my wayward brain back to the text. The deep reading that used to come naturally has become a struggle. (paragraph 2)

He concludes that the Internet "is chipping away my capacity for concentration and contemplation."

He makes this claim because the Internet invites a form of reading that was originally given the name "surfing," moving quickly over the surface; reading becomes a "power browse," a form of skimming activity that involves hopping from one source to another and rarely returning to a site that has already been visited. According to a University of London study that he cites, Internet readers rarely read more than one or two pages of an article or book before they move to another site, often saving full articles but usually not going back to read them in full. Carr also cites the work of Maryanne Wolf, a developmental psychologist and author of *Proust and Squid: The Story and Science of the Reading Brain*, who claims that this style of reading stresses "efficiency" and "immediacy"; reading online invites the quick extraction of information, but not interpretation or analysis.

This "reading" frequently goes on in an environment where multiple information sources solicit readers' attention. Recent research on multitasking suggests that those who are constantly getting information from multiple sources actually become less able to concentrate. According to one researcher, "They couldn't help thinking about the task they weren't doing. The high multitaskers are always drawing from all the information in front of them. They can't keep things separate in their minds" (Gorlick, paragraph 19). Or as Seneca wrote two millennia ago, they can't maintain a "fixed desire."

I asked my first-year college students to read Carr's essay and a response from Clay Shirky, who agrees that the transformation Carr describes is real and inevitable. But he argues that it is pointless, and often self-serving, to lament the decline of a book culture. All innovations in media transmission alter cognitive processes and raise concerns that traditional media will become obsolete (the availability of books, themselves, was a cause of concern after Gutenberg). The change we are in, according to Shirky, "isn't minor and it isn't optional"; sacrifice of older processes of communication is as inevitable as the disappearance of vinyl records and rotary phones.

A number of students fell for the bait of Carr's title—they weren't stupid because of their use of new media. Others felt that this was a generational problem for those who, unlike themselves, straddled the Internet; they grew up with computers and have difficulty imagining living without their convenience. They don't have his nostalgia for a time they never knew. But a number of students were more ambivalent about the effect of this new environment on their capacity for paying attention. Here is one full entry by one student:

> Carr was able to point out some things I hadn't even noticed about my Web-browsing habits. Besides this piece of writing, I don't remember the last time I read a whole book or article. Everything in our world is now focused on efficiency and instant gratification. Carr draws from the theory that because we research differently, we in turn think differently. The greatest evidence of the validity of his claims is in looking at our own habits. In most cases, even if subconsciously, I look for the thinking to be done for me. . . . Although I do not believe that turning back the hands of the clock, when we did not have access to the technologies, will happen, I agree with Carr in his longing for days when people spent time searching for knowledge by reading books like *War and Peace*. Part of me is also disappointed that I did not grow up in a world where I was immersing myself in books, rather than picking up an iPhone and finding the answer to anything and everything I could ever ask. I can imagine that the payoff of spending hours reading books is far greater than the hour I spend on Google for the same answer.
>
> I can safely say that I am lazy compared to a student maybe twenty years ago. I spend little time reading for pleasure, or even for information. I sift through information on the Internet, only reading the most essential fact, information, or quote, so that I can complete the assignment or task in the quickest period of time. If I didn't take the straightest path to information, I would get a much greater return. (Carly Blauvelt)

Some other students claimed that long attention spans were no longer a necessity for learning; in other words, traditional forms of reading—from beginning to end—had become inefficient:

> I agree with Carr in the sense that Google is potentially shrinking our attention span because I too find it extremely difficult to sit there and focus on a long piece of writing. In high school, when I was assigned a book, I always tried to read the actual book, but I

knew there was a three-paragraph summary online somewhere
that would give me virtually the same amount of information
but will only take me five minutes to read. (James Blouin)

One student described the actual process of distraction when he reads:

When I am reading a book, oftentimes a certain word reminds
me of a different topic. I then treat the word just like a link on
the Internet. I click it and begin thinking about something completely different. I feel like my brain is turned into a computer.
When I get on the Internet it is like entering the matrix except I
am plugging an Ethernet cable into the back of my head. I hope
I can rip these wires out one day. I want to reprogram myself to
be a reader, not a robot. (Ned McEleney)

The dirty secret about high school reading, particularly book reading, is
how much of it is faked—listen to class discussion, SparkNotes, Internet
summaries, and you can not only get by but often do well.

Researchers who track eye movements during reading on the Web
have documented what they call an "F" pattern—that is, the path of attention literally conforms to this letter shape. The top of the page is read hori-
zontally, but soon the eye drifts down vertically with few movements across
the page. As the reading progresses, the lower right corner of the page is
almost entirely ignored. Rutgers professor Mark Bauerlein concludes:

That's the drift of screen reading. Yes, it's a kind of literacy, but
it breaks down in the face of a dense argument, a Modernist
poem, a long political tract, and other texts that require steady
focus and linear attention—in a word, slow reading. Fast scanning doesn't foster flexible minds that can adapt to all kinds of
texts, and it doesn't translate into academic reading. ("Online
Literacy," paragraph 5)

This claim is consistent with research studies that find a strong correlation
between book reading and academic success—but a much weaker rela-
tion between Internet reading and achievement.

I am profoundly skeptical of claims that over the space of a couple
decades human consciousness has been so altered that reading practices

valued for centuries are suddenly unattractive or even obsolete. That in a few short years, brains are being rewired, consciousness transformed. Or that all this in inevitable and irreversible. (Even the term *rewire* belies the fact of the brain's plasticity and capacity to change as new habits are formed). These claims strike me as hubris. I can understand the attraction of imagining that one's own time on this Earth is transformative and special—I suspect that even those apocalyptic communities, the ones that wait on the crest of a hill for the end of the world, are secretly pleased that the end of the world is happening on their watch.

I recently got into an argument on this very topic. At a party, a woman asserted strongly that at no other time had people experienced so profound a change in technology and the explosion of knowledge. To be contrary (or just a jerk), I countered by saying that I would bet that the 1580s in Europe was a more disrupting time. There were, after all, the proliferation of books including heretical Bibles in the vernacular (ones you could get killed for possessing), religious wars, discoveries from "The New World," scientific research that removed the Earth from the center of the universe. Compared to these, iPods and PowerPoint seemed small potatoes. But she would have none of it. My own suspicion is that every age feels the mixture of pride and fear concerning the technological changes they see occurring around them.

I also want to speak against the technological determinism—that we are helpless to stand in the way of these alterations of cognition. Clearly traditional practices in reading are challenged by media forms that provide more immediate gratification. But the role of schools is not to capitulate, or to emulate this environment—though I am perfectly fine with using many of these tools. Still, we are not passive players in this drama. And I suspect that students don't want us to be. They come to school, or at least many do, for something that they can't get in the media environment, and I would argue that is to develop a *form of attention* that this media environment undercuts. To read a book, even one that we find intensely engaging, is still an act of perseverance; as Nancie Atwell claims, there is the need for stamina, and for patience. This is why book reading is so closely correlated with school success (Moje et al.).

Shirky argues that many of the older, more deliberate habits of reading reflect an age of "accidental scarcity" and that the reading habits of my students might be seen as the inevitable response to informational excess. There is no going back to an age of scarcity. Yet in responses like the ones I have quoted, there is not a triumphal sense of progress. There is a sense of loss, and even longing, for this capacity to read deliberately and patiently. There are reading practices that may have been born of scarcity—habits of memorization, annotation, quotation, reflection, rereading, performance—that schools should *conserve*. The danger of "accidental excess" is that language comes too cheaply.

The type of reading that my students describe is what Louise Rosenblatt calls "efferent"—a carrying away of information. Such reading is often "piecemeal," selective, a dipping in and exiting; it is basically formless, unbound, and for that reason not fully satisfying because it is removed from *patterns* of thought and feeling. Peter Elbow has argued that structure in writing is not some spatial architecture, but it invites a temporal experience; well-written texts "bind time" and carry us forward:

> Usually it is the experience of anticipation or tension that builds
> to some resolution or satisfaction. In well-structured discourse,
> music, and films (temporal media) we almost invariably see a
> pattern of alternating dissonance-and-consonance or itch and
> then scratch. Narrative is probably the most common and natu-
> ral way to set up a structure of anticipation and resolution in
> discourse. ("The Shifting," 163)

We recognize this type of temporal structure more commonly in narrative literature, but all well-structured writing, even academic writing, aims to achieve a sense of anticipation and resolution: There is a problem that needs explanation and resolution, a contest of opposing positions; there is a plot, an invitation to "follow me." To be sure, students can experience this movement in other media, as Elbow notes, but when reading is piecemeal, removed from any sense of undergoing this temporal structure, it loses a primary appeal and becomes thinly functional. That's what I suspect some of my students were saying they had lost.

I realize that my emphasis on slowness will be taken as a last-gasp humanist plea for literary reading when much of the workplace reading must be quick and efficient. But even in our encounters with highly trained professionals, doing practical work, I am convinced that speed leads to inefficiency. I was speaking recently with my physician who for years chafed under the time pressure and accountability measures of the local hospital that owned his practice. "You know, I see hundreds of patients with headaches each year. And in almost all cases, the problems take care of themselves. They aren't dangerous. But maybe once a year, that headache is caused by a brain tumor. I have to keep that possibility open." In his book, *How Doctors Think*, Jerome Groopman describes a process called "anchoring," or confirmation bias, in which the doctor quickly comes to a diagnosis and removes the very uncertainty that my doctor spoke of. Instead of attending to and integrating the key, possibly discrepant kinds of information, the doctor cherry-picks information that confirms the "anchored" predisposition (65). The individuality and specificity of the ailment is dissolved into a category—then there is a scripted decision tree of treatments. It is not difficult to imagine how the sense of "being on the clock" can promote this thinking.

Which leads me to my encounters with a sleep specialist. (I will try to keep medical details to a minimum, so this doesn't become what my students call an "overshare.") About a year ago, my wife urged me to be checked out for sleep apnea; I got a referral to a physician specializing in sleep disorders, who ordered a sleep study. This turned out to be one of the most bizarre nights of my life. It took place in a windowless room of a local hospital, which looked like a Motel 8. When I began to feel sleepy, an attendant began hooking me up, wires everywhere, attached to my legs, chest, head, a tube under my nose—all of these wires connected to a huge necklace on my chest. On the ceiling of the room, there was a small glass globe that contained a camera that would film me all evening, all monitored in a control room. My only job was to *sleep*. For a person with sleeping problems to begin with, this was not easy. This hugely expensive process depended on me sleeping, and I could feel that familiar cycle—trying to sleep keeping me from sleeping.

As you can imagine, all this monitoring produced a lot of data, a five-page report with graphs,
pie charts, and tables (and here we begin to get to
the reading part). At my follow-up appointment, I
could see my physician spend about a minute outside the examination room looking over this report, circling a few numbers. I remember thinking,
"All those wires for this reading." I could feel myself
becoming a category. He came into the examining
room and explained that I had a severe sleep disor-
der, which would necessitate another sleep study to
fit me for a CPAP (continuous positive airway pressure) machine—and to come back after I had tried it
for a month. On my way out, I asked for a copy of the
sleep study.

There is a sense of loss, even longing, for this capacity to read deliberately and patiently.

About six weeks later, I had a follow-up visit, and
I told him that I found the CPAP breathing machine intolerable; the air
forced into my lungs made me nauseous, and the idea of being hooked up
this way for the rest of my life, to have my sleep mechanized, was simply
too depressing. He began to explain an alternative: surgery (actually two
surgeries) to reconstruct my breathing passage. This sounded even worse.
Then I pulled out the sleep study results, which I had read as carefully as I
could. I pointed out that almost all of the apnea "events" occurred when I
was sleeping on my back (only one-sixth of my total sleeping time—about
an hour). When I slept on my side, it seemed there were no episodes. I
asked, "If I could find a way to avoid sleeping on my back, wouldn't that
solve the problem?"

I showed the report with his circling and pointed to the table I was
referring to. He looked it over, and agreed, "Yes, the numbers for sleeping
on the side are normal." Then, to his great credit, he said, "You know, people have tried a kind of Pavlovian approach." (I was thinking "Pavlov, now
we're getting somewhere.") "They might sew tennis balls into the back of
a shirt, which keeps them off their back." I could tell this would not be his
choice, but he put it out there. And so I bought some tennis balls (Penn

Championship—extra-duty felt), and my wife created a Velcro pocket in the back of some athletic T-shirts. It seems to work.

The Pleasures of Scarcity

When I was ten, I had a short but memorable conversation with my father. As I recall, I was eating potato chips at the time—Ohio's own Jones' Potato Chips—by the fistful. Knowing the way I ate (and still eat), there were surely crumbs down my shirt. My dad looked on with an expression somewhere between amusement and disapproval. "You know," he said, "when I was growing up we got a small bag of them once a year, around Christmas time." He had grown up in an orphanage in Tiffin, and I could imagine the boys of his cottage lined up to get this annual treat.

I suppose the "message" was to be appreciative—that I was lucky, lucky to be living in the relatively affluent 1950s, lucky to have parents providing for me. But my feeling was the opposite: I thought potato chips could never taste as good to me as they did to him that one day of the year.

There can be no reverse time machine to this time, and I doubt if I would want to get on it if there were. But scarcity can foster an appreciation just as affluence and excess can dull the appetite. Can lemonade or raisins ever taste as good to us as they did to young Frank McCourt? By extension, can reading ever be as sweet or concentrated as it was when books were rare, when for centuries in Western culture the Bible was an inexhaustible source of meaning and inspiration, when the first collections of poetry were call *treasuries*? When reading invariably meant rereading, and re-rereading (something young children instinctively understand). The fifteenth-century Catholic monk, Thomas à Kempis, had this to say about reading:

> [Take] a book into thine hands as Simeon the Just took the Child Jesus into his arms to carry him and kiss him. And thou hast finished reading, close the book and give thanks for every word out of the mouth of God; because in the Lord's field thou has found a hidden treasure. (Quoted in Manguel 14–15)

Not exactly an invitation to speed-reading.

My title for this book mirrors the concept of Slow Food. The analogy is not precise—books are not food, reading is not eating, growing is not writing. But there is something there. In "fast-food nation," quantity tops quality; local culture vanishes; we are cut off from the production and cooking of our food; and we lose touch with the resourcefulness of earlier generations (that's where the term "home *economics*" comes from). I learned a lot from my neighbor Minnie Mae Murray, wife of the noted writing specialist Don Murray, who lived across the street from me. Like my own parents, she grew up during the Depression and nothing went to waste—chicken bones became broth, leftover meat and vegetables became soups and stews, what couldn't be used became compost for gardens. Early in their marriage, she grew pole beans so high she had to get on Don's shoulders to pick them. This was the kind of neighborhood I grew up in, a small Ohio town where most of our older neighbors had grown up on farms. We all grew gardens, and late in the summer Collie Weaver would come by with a couple of homegrown cantaloupes. We would eat the tomatoes from our own gardens, still warm from the late summer sun. This is more than nostalgia—it is a glimpse of a more sustainable, healthy, and pleasurable relationship to food.

In the same way, we can reclaim resourceful modes of reading, born in times of scarcity. We can learn to pay attention, concentrate, devote ourselves to authors. We can slow down so we can hear the voice of texts, feel the movement of sentences, experience the pleasure of words—and own passages that speak to us.

We can adopt the turtle, slow but perennially victorious, as our emblem.

Six Practices

1. **Performing**—attending to the texts as dramatic, as enacted for an audience (even internally). Special attention is paid to acoustic and emotional qualities of language: emphasis, pace, voices of narrator, and characters.

2. **Memorizing**—learning "by heart." Retaining word-for-word memories of passages that serve as frames for perceiving experience.

3. **Centering**—assigning significance to a part of text, often literally making a mark to indicate an act of attention.

4. **Problem finding**—interrupting the flow of reading to note a problem or confusion, and then adopting strategies to deal with the problem.

5. **Reading like a writer**—attending to the decisions a writer makes. This may consist of acts of specific appreciation for mentor texts—or in considering alternatives and revisions.

6. **Elaborating**—developing the capacity to comment and expand upon texts, sometimes referred to as "opening a text."

Chapter 3

READING GOES SILENT
PERFORMING

The ear is the only true writer and the only true reader. I know
people who read without hearing the sentence sounds and they
were the fastest readers. Eye readers we call them. They get the
meaning by glances. But they are bad readers because they miss the
best part of what a good writer puts into his work.

—ROBERT FROST

I am holding in my hand a copy of the Fifth McGuffey Reader, published
in 1879, and, judged by the inscriptions, owned at one point by one Allice
(she also spells her name Alice) Moore (also Moor) of Findlay, Ohio, and by
George Jenkins, who dates his signature 1891. One of them did a series of
drawings, presumably of their teacher, large but undefined bodice, narrow waist, hair elaborately coiled at the top and back of her head. In one
drawing, she wears an elaborate bustle skirt of stripes and spots, small
high-heeled shoes, and a carefully drawn Victorian high collar. Her finger
is pointing and her mouth is clearly open—singing, giving directions?

I expect that for many the definition of reading at the beginning of the
book would seem as outdated as this teacher's Victorian dress:

> The great object to be accomplished in reading as a rhetorical
> exercise is to convey to the hearer, fully and clearly, the ideas
> and feelings of the writer. (9)

The reader, as imagined by the writers of this text, was an "oral" reader, a performer. Reading was a public, even communal activity—a "rhetorical" practice. Other elocutionary readers of this period came with illustrations of hand motions and body positions—for example, "The active and passive chest." The Fifth McGuffey begins with a brief introduction to key elocutionary concepts: pitch, inflection, various degrees of emphasis, the dangers of reading in a monotone. The practical value of this oral skill is demonstrated in the first complete selection, entitled "The Ideal Reader."

This fictional story takes place in the court of Frederick the Great, King of Prussia in the eighteenth century. Frederick has just returned from a hunting trip, and because his eyes were "dazzled" by the sun, he has difficulty reading a petition from a widower (her husband had been killed in battle), pleading that her only son, who was in delicate health, be spared military service. The King asks one of his pages to read. He fails miserably, reading in a monotone, without pausing as if the petition were one long word. The King stops him. "Is it an auctioneer's list of goods to be sold you are hurrying through?" He asks the second page, who errs in the opposite direction, emphasizing every word, prolonging the articulation of every syllable. He too is stopped. "Are you reciting a lesson in elementary sounds?" He is about to send them both away, until he spots a young girl, the daughter of one of the laborers in the royal garden, and asks her to read to him.

So here enters the heroine of the tale, Ernestine. The King gives her the petition, and she skims the opening lines to get a sense of the content. At this point, surprised by the delay, he asks, "What is the matter? Don't you know how to read?" She assures him that she does and proceeds to read "with so much feeling, and with an articulation so pure and distinct" that when she finishes, King Frederick is moved to tears:

> Oh! now I understand what it is all about; but I never would
> have known, certainly I never would have felt, its meaning had
> I trusted to these young gentlemen, whom I now dismiss from
> my service for one year, advising them to occupy the time in
> learning to read. (41–42)

In true Horatio Alger fashion, this one act of reading works wonders: The waiver of military services is granted; the woman's son is invited to paint a likeness of the king and becomes a celebrated artist; Ernestine's father becomes chief gardener; Ernestine is given support to continue her education. And the poor pages, they too rose to prominence after their year of study—and they owed it all to "their good elocution."

I imagine that even students in the late 1800s found some of this heavy-handed and old-fashioned. In the interests of accuracy, I must report that Ernestine herself was so moved by the mother's petition that her breast (singular) did indeed "heave." But I would like to argue that this vision of reading is particularly expansive and worth recuperating. Competent reading, according to this parable, is deliberate; indeed, Ernestine takes so much time that the king thinks she can't read. What we would now call "comprehension" (or test as comprehension) is part, *but only part*, of the activity of reading. Her reading is successful because the king could both understand and feel the meaning of the petition. This was possible because Ernestine, in those moments of delay, had made an emotional connection with the woman and her plea (yes, her eyes "began to glisten"). This emotional meaning, this rhetorical effect, is intimately linked to the acoustical properties of the language—the way it cues emphasis, pitch, pauses. Her reading is truly fluent because she is sensitive to the sound system cued by the writer.

While in practice these readings may have been bombastic or mawkish, there was a robust conception of reading behind these practices, as described by Frank Spaulding and Catherine Bryce, authors of the popular early twentieth-century series, The Aldine Readers:

> Dramatizing is complete reading. Dramatizing is, indeed, more than mere preparation for reading; dramatizing is reading in the fullest sense. Instead of simply thinking and picturing in their imagination the thoughts and ideas of the printed page, the pupils, in dramatizing, make those thoughts and ideas live. . . . They feel as well as understand. (In Bianchi, 29)[1]

This statement is entirely consistent with the conception of reading put forward by Robert Frost at about the same time: "Everything written is as good as it is dramatic. It need not declare itself in form, but it is drama or

---

1. I am indebted to Lisa Bianchi for uncovering these arguments for silent reading, and for her passionate case for performance as a mode of comprehension.

it is nothing. By whom, where, and when is the question" (in Poirier, 452).

These sound cues also enable readers to connect, to imagine, the presence of the writer, a quality writers often refer to as *voice*. The great literary critic Richard Poirier describes a radical literature course he taught at Harvard early in his career, one that broke away from the fashionable New Critical view of literature as architectural, spatial, structure; no, he argued, reading is an experience in time, an unfolding:

> *"Everything written is as good as it is dramatic."*
>
> *—Robert Frost*

> Reading must be actively synchronized with the generative energies of the writing itself. It is not enough to understand what is said, since this is less than what is being expressed. (441)

This spatial perspective, with its emphasis on decoding imagery patterns, represented to him the unfortunate triumph of the eye over the ear. The course Poirier taught was looked down upon by other graduate students and theoretically sophisticated junior faculty:

> Understandably so, since we taught students to respond to those inflections of language which most teachers of literature, even as they dig away at metaphoric patterns, often cannot hear or which they ignore. (445)

It may seem a long distance between Ernestine's heaving breast and Poirier's Harvard literature class, but in both cases two things are clear: (1) reading is more than the comprehension ("to understand" is not enough) and (2) a full response requires sensitivity to the acoustical properties of language.

Even something as "mechanical" as punctuation helps in this reconstruction. For example, here is Joel Conarroe's appreciation of the way *New Yorker* writer Roger Angell regulates pace in his many baseball pieces:

> Mr. Angell is addicted to dashes and parentheses—small pauses or digressions in the narrative like those moments when the umpire dusts off home plate or a pitcher rubs up a new ball— that serve to slow an already deliberate movement almost to a standstill. (In Lunsford, Ruszkiewicz, and Walters, 377)

Although students are often taught punctuation as one more set of rules, as one more set of snares that writing sets before them, it is really a set of opportunities for creating a sense of style, of making our personal *mark*. Fran Lebowitz explains it this way:

> In conversation you can use timing, a look, inflection, pauses. But on the page all you have is commas, dashes, and the amount of syllables in a word. When I write I read everything out loud to get the right rhythm.

Punctuation slows things down and indicates degrees of pauses (significantly the British call the period a "full stop"). Dashes and parentheses allow us to bring in additional information either quietly as an aside (parentheses) or loudly and with emphasis—the dash. Commas are somewhere in between. Inevitably, the faster a reader processes text, the more they read in what Robert Frost called "glances," the more they have to override systems of punctuation and ignore the rhythmic cues of the writer.

Paradoxically, we seek out a teller, a connection to an oral tradition, even as we read silently. That is why writers like Richard Ford will painstakingly read their full manuscripts aloud to test them for the way they sound—*even though his readers may not read one word aloud*. In the movie *Shadowlands*, the C. S. Lewis character asks an undergraduate why we should read literature. The student struggles with a couple of possibilities, which Lewis rejects, and then provides his answer, "We read to know we are not alone." Tracy Kidder describes the connection this way:

> I think one of the things that gives pleasure in reading—at least gives me pleasure in reading—is the sense of the presence of a storyteller, whether it's fiction or nonfiction. I think we can use a term like "voice" or "style," but a large part of it is the sense that there's someone behind the scenes adroitly pulling the strings, the reader's realizing with pleasure that there's someone there.

Henry David Thoreau makes the same point in the opening to *Walden* where he justifies his use of the first person: "We commonly do not remember that it is, after all, always the first person that is speaking." (It's revealing that he uses the word *speaking* when he is referring to written text.)

I remember vividly my own first experience of this storytelling presence—the first time I became acutely aware of a writer's voice, one that seemed to speak directly to me. I was in eighth grade and home from school with the flu, bored, eating saltine crackers and drinking 7-Up on a Friday afternoon. The three TV channels carried soap operas, which have never interested me (I tell my kids that *in my day* I had to walk all the way to the television to change channels). I remember staring at the ceiling trying to count the perforations in the ceiling tiles (22 × 22). About midafternoon, my father came home from Ashland College and I'm sure I made him aware of my boredom. As usual he began cleaning the house as he always did on Friday. He started in the upstairs, and he called down to me, suggesting I read a book that was making the rounds among his friends. "Just start it," he said, "read to me the first page out loud." The book was a thirty-five-cent paperback with a cover picture of a high school–aged boy with an overcoat and a weird hunting hat on—and an odd title, *Catcher in the Rye*. So I began:

> If you really want to hear about it, the first thing you'll probably want to know is where I was born, and what my lousy childhood was like, and how my parents were occupied and all before they had me, and all that David Copperfield kind of crap, but I don't feel like going into it, if you want to know the truth. In the first place, that stuff bores me, and in the second place, my parents would have two hemorrhages apiece if I told anything pretty personal about them. They're quite touchy about anything like that, especially my father. They're *nice* and all—I'm not saying that—but they're also touchy as hell. (Salinger, 3)

I remember stopping after "David Copperfield kind of crap." Maybe embarrassed to be reading this to my father, but also just loving the freedom of the speaker, the way I *heard* him, as if the book were solely intended for *me*; I loved his edginess and irreverence (and profanity)—and would continue to hear him as I moved into the book, right to the end when he speaks of missing all the people he had written about. I write this days after J. D. Salinger's death, and I realize that my experience of these sentences was shared by millions of his readers.

I'm convinced that most nonreaders have never had such a moment. I notice that many of my students refer to the author of a book as "they"— as if the book was not actually written, but produced or manufactured by a conglomerate that inflicted reading on them. Contrary to what C. S. Lewis claimed, for them reading is a lonely, silent, asocial activity. A void. Boring. Time stolen from activities they would prefer to be doing:

> I never did enjoy pleasure reading. I just get tired and sleepy and my mind gets to wandering somewhere out there in left field. I come back to read a bit more, and then I go into this grey area and I'm back in left field again. I get tired. I say, "Why am I doing this?" and I go do something else. (Rosenthal, 37)

They have trouble imagining what keeps readers voluntarily engaged with books:

> I guess people who read all the time must get something out of it that I just haven't experienced. They must take the material and really understand it. I don't know whether they force themselves to read or not. (Rosenthal, 35)

I suspect that many of these nonreaders are "overmatched" by the books they are assigned—the sheer length, unfamiliarity, vocabulary demands, and expected pace for reading intimidate them. Researchers in comprehension would also say that these nonreaders cannot (or do not) employ the active strategies that successful readers routinely use—such as asking questions, predicting, visualizing, making inferences, assigning significance. To this list I would add what I can only awkwardly call *auditorizing*, creating an internal sense of the sound of the language, developing an inner ear for the way writing is *told*. For these readers, silent reading is truly silent—a dead space with no narrative attraction, no connection—which is why they drift off into "left field." They regularly speak of how easily distracted they are. The text has no hold on them. But if writers go to such pains to create these acoustical properties of voice, it makes sense that they expect readers to register those properties, even if they never read a single word aloud. If writers orchestrate their writing with punctuation, they expect that orchestration to be re-created in reading. For the fact is that many of these nonreaders thoroughly enjoy listening to the books they reject—when they are read aloud well. And in my experience, they engage in many of these comprehension strategies when they can hear the text.

The Rise of Silent Reading

Although silent reading is the norm today, for most of the history of literacy oral reading has predominated. Such reading was often employed with sacred texts that required the full involvement of the reader:

> In sacred texts, where every letter and the number of letters and their order were dictated by the godhead, full comprehension required not only the eyes but the rest of the body: swaying to the cadence of the sentences and lifting to one's lips the holy words, so that nothing of the divine could be lost in the reading. (Manguel, 45–46)

Anything the mind could process had a "physical reality in sounds" (47). However, the practice of silent reading was not unknown in classical times—there is an instance of Alexander the Great reading a letter, silently, much to the amazement of onlookers. One of the most famous encounters in reading history occurred in 383 AD when a young professor of rhetoric, who would later become St. Augustine, was offered a teaching position in Milan. While there, he sought out a very popular ascetic preacher, Ambrose, who would also be canonized. Ambrose spent a great deal of time reading alone in his small cell, and this is where Augustine encountered him:

> When he read [Augustine writes] his eyes scanned the page and his heart sought out the meaning, but his voice was silent and his tongue was still. Anyone could approach him freely and guests were not commonly announced, so that, often, when we came to visit him, we found him reading like this in silence for he never read aloud. (In Manguel, 42)

Augustine's astonishment is evident by the fact that he reiterates *four times* in this short observation that Ambrose was reading silently.

It was not until the ninth century AD that silent reading became the norm, facilitated by the emerging practice of putting spaces between letters and of modifying the writing of Latin to emphasize word order. Both of these innovations allowed for scanning ahead and taking in larger "chunks" of texts (Saenger). Scribes in monasteries were enjoined to do their work silently. And with silent reading came the possibility of a kind of individuality that was not possible when reading was communal and oral. In these oral settings, an authority could monitor interpretations and enforce orthodox reading. But silent reading allowed for a new relationship between writer and reader—which is why the translating and printing of Bibles in the vernacular was so threatening to the Catholic church in the fifteenth and sixteenth centuries.

> With silent reading the reader was at last able to establish an un-
> restricted relationship with the book and the words. The words
> no longer needed to occupy the time required to pronounce
> them. They could exist in interior space, rushing on or barely
> begun, fully deciphered or only half-said, while the reader's
> thoughts inspected them at leisure, drawing new notions from
> them, allowing comparisons from memory and other books left
> open for simultaneous perusal. The reader had time to consider
> and reconsider the precious words whose sounds—he now
> knew—could echo as well within as without. (Manguel, 50–51)

Two things stand out in this elegant description. One is his claim that in silent reading, the sound of language is not necessarily lost; it can be re-created within. The other is that Manguel sees one advantage of silent reading to be the possibility of *slowing down*, contemplating, comparing. But this argument was turned on its head during the great debate about silent reading in U.S. schools.

This battle over silent reading was played out in the early part of the twentieth century. One key factor was the rise of educational measurements that formed the backbone of experimental research in reading. The most famous test of this period was carried out by Robert Yerkes and measured the mental ages of recruits to the U.S. Army during the First World War. Reading proficiency was a key element of this assessment—which showed a huge number of these recruits were severely retarded in their mental growth. He reported that 70 percent had a mental age less than 15 years. Although historians of assessment such as Stephen Gould have virtually discredited this test and the claims made, it led to one of the periodic educational crises in American education. What was the cause of this poor performance?

The answer, researchers claimed, was the fossilized approaches to reading that stressed oral performance at the expense of reading for meaning or, as it was called then, "thought-getting." Students had to be liberated from a system of instruction that tied reading so closely to the "sound" of language (sometimes making an exception for poetry). John O'Brien, author of *Silent Reading: With Special Reference to Methods for Developing Speed*, summarized this position:

> Unless the finding of the psychological laboratory and of the
> experimental investigations can be adapted to development
> of practical methods of classroom procedure, the teaching of
> reading will be in the future, as it has been in the past, the slow,
> mechanical, oral type, unbenefited and unimproved by all the
> discoveries of scientific research. (31)

O'Brien identified three kinds of readers—motor, auditory, and visual readers—in ascending levels of proficiency. The motor readers physically formed words, through lip movements and subvocalizations, a process that O'Brien claimed wasted energy and created a disparity between the pace of vocal reading and the faster movement of the eye.

The auditory reader occupied a kind of middle ground and could be a fairly skilled reader. Norman Lewis, in his popular 1944 book, *How to Read Better and Faster*, describes this reader:

> His speed is not unduly hampered, for he is not actually pro-
> nouncing the words he "hears," but only imagining their pro-
> nunciation. Only a *small* part of his mind is involved with the
> sound of the words; but small as it may be, by just so much is he
> retarding comprehension. (206)

The visual reader has mastered the "art of reading," by silencing the text, by not converting symbols to sound even internally: "We may say, in a sense, that he doesn't read at all but *absorbs,* in the same effortless, unconscious, efficient manner that a dry sponge absorbs water" (206). Lewis admits that this elimination of sound is difficult even for his City College students:

> "But I *hear* the words I read." The complaint is genuine and oc-casionally a little desperate. My only honest answer can be: "Of course you do. Almost all readers but the very rapid and very skillful do. But don't worry. As your speed and skill increase, you will hear them less and less." (207)

Some of the strategies for suppressing vocalization in children must strike us today as barbaric. Here is one proposed by Luella Cole in her book, *Improvement of Reading*:

> The first, and by far the simplest, means of bringing about this result is to render the speech mechanism incapable of pronouncing words, even partially. A simple and effective means of bringing about this result is to have the child put two fingers into his mouth, using them to separate the upper and lower teeth and to hold down the tongue. Nobody can articulate words with the mouth hanging open. If the child, through force of habit, moves his jaws to articulate, he bites his fingers. (89)

Cole also tells the story of one child under her instruction who devised his own means of suppressing sound: He brought to school a "neatly whittled and sandpapered piece of wood" wrapped in a handkerchief. He placed this piece of wood in his mouth and bit on it as he read, eliminating any possibility of vocalization. Not all of Cole's interventions were this dra-matic; she also recommends that children chew gum while they read—the chewing also interferes with vocalization. But she cautions gum chewing should not become a habit and should be discontinued when the habit of vocalization was broken. All of these interventions, it should be noted, were firmly rooted in the science of the time.

Coles is categorical in claiming that reading is—or should be—an entirely visual process; any reversion to sound interferes with the more robust and efficient process, as if a thoroughbred is attached to a farm wagon:

> Since the eyes almost inevitably move too fast, they get ahead of the voice once or twice in every line. He must bring them back to the word he is pronouncing—thus causing a regression. (62)

Any attention to the sound dimensions of written language, even inner speech, is disruptive and inefficient.

The most prominent researcher of the period, Edward Thorndike, studied eye movements during silent reading, and demonstrated how in silent reading the eyes take in chunks of text as they move in leaps or saccades. Edmund Huey, in his 1921 summary of reading research, claimed that oral reading had a ceiling of about four words/second, although silent readers could process texts at two or three times that rate (Cole would claim four times)—with no diminishment of comprehension. It was time, he argued, for reading to go silent and become "thought-getting"; he advocated "visual reading, omitting this complex functioning of speech" as the most "economical" use of time and energy (10). For Huey, like O'Brien and Cole, almost any attention to sound slowed reading, detracted from comprehension—and the reforms in reading that advocated silent reading would produce "definite savings of time, money, health, and definite improvements in mental habits" (431). The order of this list is, I think, significant. It demonstrates a link to the spirit of "scientific management" and "the cult of efficiency" that Chaplin satirized.

He placed this piece of wood in his mouth and bit on it as he read, eliminating any possibility of vocalization.

Reading, in the end, is another form of production, and oral reading habits failed to produce as many words/minute as silent reading methods. There is rarely the hint, in the writing of these reformers, that something might be lost in the switch.

Take for example one lesson in silent reading for third-grade students described in a 1925 issue of the *Teacher's College Record* in which the teacher began to read a passage aloud from a student textbook, then stopped to have students read silently and answer questions. The teacher's job was to calculate their reading speed. Here are the directions to the teacher:

> Regulate your speed of reading so that the last word on page 9 will be read just as the minute hand of the watch is at some ten second point. At the expiration of the first ten seconds write the number 10 on the blackboard. At the expiration of twenty seconds erase the 10 and write 20. Continue similarly until all pupils have finished. (Dransfield, 747)

As I imagine this environment for third graders taking the test, there must have been an unnerving flurry of sounds, of erasings and chalk on blackboard—*every ten seconds*—as they read "on the clock." After the reading they were asked twenty true-or-false questions.

Whatever we might think of these practices, reformers like Thorndike, Huey, and Coles pose a significant challenge to earlier oral reading practices. If efficient reading involved a shift to a strictly visual system, much of my argument is undermined. It would follow that any attention to the oral dimensions of written texts would hold the reader back and interfere with comprehension. If the eye moved in saccades, taking in visual chunks of text, what value is there in attending to sound at all?

The response is that *even silent reading does not rely on a purely visual system for meaning.* Silent reading is not truly silent; it depends on intonation. Obviously in oral language, intonation is closely connected to meaning, as Peter Elbow eloquently observes:

> When we hear natural appropriate intonation, we get the gift of *hearing meaning* as opposed to having to construct meaning; the music of intonation enacts a rhythm and melody of meaning. As listeners, we often feel as though the speaker and the language are doing the work of getting meaning in our heads. (*Vernacular*, 93ms)

Skilled speakers use emphasis and the slight pauses within sentences that keep us with them; they help us process meaning as they convey it. They appropriately break language into what are called "intonation units." The problem with the "motormouth" is that he or she fails to do this, and even though sentences may be clear and coherent, we have trouble processing them as listeners.

The saccades of the eye correspond to intonational boundaries. One obvious example is the period: The saccade would not leap over the sentence boundary and straddle two sentences. Punctuation was invented to signal some of the intonational work that the reader is expected to perform. Effective writers, Elbow argues, make use of "intonational" instincts that they learn from speaking and listening; there is a coordination between intonational patterns and the natural "leaping" activity of the eye. By contrast, we often struggle to pay attention to texts that violate the speechlike rhythms that make for ready comprehension (academic papers are often a culprit). It is physically wearying to spend much time with this kind of prose. So reading never goes totally silent—or if it does, we have tremendous difficulty processing it.

The volumes of *Teachers College Record* from this period report regularly on the work of Thorndike and Arthur Gates, whose reading test is still in use in schools. We can see the beginning of comprehension tests that presented the student with paragraphs of increasing difficulty followed by comprehension questions, still the standard format of reading comprehension texts and memorable to anyone who attended school in the 1970s and worked through the colors of the SRA kits. The message was clear—reading achievement was not a mystical capability, but a form of cognition, a solitary and measurable capacity. As Thorndike put it:

> Education is one form of human engineering and will profit by measurements of human nature as mechanical and electrical engineering have profited by using foot-pound, calorie, volt, and ampere. (371)

Thorndike compressed this position to an elegant statement: "Whatever exists, exists in some amount" (379). The tests designed by Thorndike and others were essential for the scientific management of schools, described in chilling terms by one of the dominant educators of the time, Ellwood P. Cubberley:

> Our schools are, in a sense, factories in which the raw prod-ucts (children) are to be shaped and fashioned into products to meet the various demands of life. The specification for manufacturing come from the demands of twentieth century civilization, and it is the business of the school to build pupils to the specifications laid down. This demands good tools, spe-cialized machinery, continuous measurement of production to see if it is according to specifications, and the elimination of waste in manufacture, and a large variety of output. (In Callahan, 97)

The "objective" tests of Gates and Thorndike provided key measure-ment tools.

This "text plus questions" format became so ubiquitous that reading selections seemed naked, and uninstructive, without them. There was an agenda for the reading, and someone other than the reader was making the agenda, determining what was significant. (By contrast, the McGuffey Readers I've seen did not contain comprehension questions or come with a teacher's manual.) Advocates of silent reading monitored by ques-tions promoted what they called "thought-getting," an interesting turn of phrase. Not "thought-making" but "thought-getting"—as if the "thought" were in the text to be "gotten." And that's the way it was presented to my generation of readers. The "main idea" was *in* the text as surely as a plum has a pit. Key details were determined not by the interests and purposes of the reader, and not by the author, but by those who created the apparatus around the passage. I came to hate those questions because I felt I was reading for someone else—and I was.

These reforms also promoted what Louise Rosenblatt called an "ef-ferent" emphasis in reading—where the function of texts is to transmit information. Reading that focused on "thought-getting" seemed to resem-ble very closely the functional, dispassionate kind of tasks that appear on reading tests, as Thorndike describes:

In school practices it appears likely that exercises in silent reading to find the answers to given questions, or give a summary of the matter read, or list questions which it answers should in large measure replace oral reading. (333)

This view of texts, in which all aesthetic appeal is stripped, is light-years away from Frost's claim that reading "is drama or it is nothing" (in Poirier, 452). Even literary texts came to be treated as repositories of testable information—leading to Rosenblatt's wickedly appropriate title for one of her essays: "What Facts Does This Poem Teach You?"

This "efferent" functional view of reading is evident in recent attempts to define the features of a "considerate" text. Normally these features are thought to be clear text structures, subheadings, directly stated main ideas, key transitional terms, and an awareness of the informational needs of the reader. As significant as these qualities surely are, lists like this seem technical and incomplete to me—even antiseptic, an example of what is now called "cold cognition." They overrate the effectiveness of logic and rationality, and fail to account for what truly holds a reader to text (even nonfictional ones) and keeps him or her reading.

Even so-called formal writing benefits from the use of some oral strategies. . . .

To this list I would add that considerate texts "address" the reader; they convey the presence of a teller, they are connected to the oral tradition from which writing evolved. This presence may not be marked by a literal *I* in the writing, but it is often felt as what I would call *cognitive energy*, a palpable sense of a writerly mind at work, narrating, questioning, debating, asserting, sometimes belittling, sometimes qualifying in midsentence, occasionally springing a surprise. Call it "attitude." Many of these markers of writerly presence involve the intermixture of oral language features, all of which contribute to what is often loosely called "voice."

Even so-called formal writing benefits from the use of some oral strategies (such as my use of *so-called* in this sentence). In fact, we all—even as experienced and competent readers—have difficulty sustaining attention when these features are removed or avoided by "serious" or indifferent writers. Clive James, referring to the writing in Leonid Brezhnev's memoirs, describes this deadness well:

> Here is a book so dull that a whirling dervish could read himself
> to sleep with it. If you were to recite even a single page in the
> open air, birds would fall out of the sky and dogs drop dead. (In
> Buckley, 10)

Our bodies are our first-alert system: we yawn, feel a heaviness, lose our place, check the number of pages to go, and sigh.

Good Reads

In the mid 1970s, I visited a number of British secondary schools in Manchester, Birmingham, and Leeds. Most were reasonably orderly, and I felt welcome. But one stood out as different. It was an all-boys school in Birmingham, located in a dismal housing project built after World War II, a set of high-rise buildings with no variation. The school itself felt crowded and unruly. As an outsider, I felt myself the object of attention. Boys would come up to me and ask a cheeky question, "Sir, in America, . . . ?" And they would giggle and snicker. It was one of the only schools I visited where the teachers' room seemed a safe haven from the chaos outside. I met there with the teacher whose class I was about to visit—a large third-form (about ninth-grade) group. I asked him what he planned on doing, and he said he'd begin by reading from *Portrait of the Artist as a Young Man*. For the life of me I couldn't imagine James Joyce succeeding in this school, but I followed him into his classroom filled with over thirty boys. They settled down and he began to read the section where Stephen is beaten by the Father Dolan, the Prefect of Studies, because his glasses are broken and he can't do his lessons. The teacher had the bullying voice of Father Dolan down perfectly:

> —Out here, Dedalus, Lazy little schemer. I see schemer in your
> face. Where did you break your glasses?

Dolan dismisses Stephen's explanation that they were broken during recess on the cinder path, and he orders him to hold out his hand for a beating.

> Stephen closed his eyes and held out in the air his trembling hand with the palm upwards. He felt the prefect of studies touch it for a moment at the fingers to straighten it and then the swish of the soutane as the pandybat was lifted to strike. A hot burning stinging tingling blow like the loud crack of a broken stick made his trembling hand crumple together like a leaf in the fire: and at the sound and the pain scalding tears were driven into his eyes. His whole body was shaking with fright, his arm was shaking and his crumpled burning livid hand shook like a loose leaf in the air. (50)

The class of boys was transfixed as he read; they were stunned into seriousness right up until Father Dolan's exit:

> Father Dolan will be in every day to see if any boy, any idle little loafer needs flogging. Every day. Every day. (51)

When he had finished the reading, this teacher asked students to think about times they were punished, fairly or unfairly, or hurt—and to write as much as they could remember about the experience. And it worked. The excerpt from *Portrait* served the double purpose of prompting memory and providing a model of how we might write about that memory—as if we are stealing energy from the excerpt. The effectiveness was dependent, totally dependent, on the oral reading of the piece. As I was leaving the classroom I congratulated him on the success of the lesson and asked what he was doing next.

"I think I'll try Dostoevsky." I felt my skepticism return, Dostoevsky with this group? "Yes, Dostoevsky, remember the dream in *Crime and Punishment* where the donkey is beaten?" I did know that scene of almost unimaginable graphic cruelty and I said, "That just might work."

In visits to British classrooms, I noticed several things about reading aloud to students. First, teachers were generally good at it—they rehearsed and could be appropriately dramatic. They provided a model of the way good writing can sound, the rhythms and emphases that McGuffey felt were so important for "ideal" reading. I am convinced that such reading is critical in helping students create the internal performances that good literature invites us to create (young children often develop a "reading voice" before they can read). Second, this oral reading continued in later grades to a greater degree than it seemed to in U.S. schools. And finally, teachers were more willing to use excerpts of great literature that students would probably be unable to cope with if they were reading entire works, particularly reading silently. Oral reading was a manageable bridge to these authors—they became accessible, even powerful in small, oral doses. Some students might later meet up with them in subsequent classes, but for all students in this class James Joyce was now more than a name.

Even as experienced readers, we can benefit by the oral readings of skilled performers who can help us internalize a voice for the text. This occurred for me recently as I was about to teach Walt Whitman in a graduate course, including his famous poem "Crossing Brooklyn Ferry." It failed to make an impression on me as I read it, and I had trouble imagining why it was so praised—until I heard Chris Cooper read it on a PBS special on Whitman:

> It avails not, time or place—distance avails not,
> I am with you, you men and women of a generation, or ever
>   so many generations hence,
> Just as you feel when you look on the river and sky, so I felt,
> Just as any of you is one of the living crowd, I was one of a
>   crowd.
> Just as you are refresh'd by the gladness of the river and the
>   bright flow, I was refreshed (145)

It is difficult to describe Cooper's voice, but it was much slower than I imagined when reading the lines silently; the pauses at the end of the lines gave space for reflection. Whitman often celebrated loitering and lounging, not being hurried—the lines felt at ease and calm, and deeply reassuring as if Whitman is expressing a loyalty and identification with all generations—"I am with you." As he claimed to span centuries, past and present—he had "all the time in the world."

This pattern of reading excerpts from favorite writers has become part of my repertoire. One of my favorites is Calvin Trillin's essay, "The Best Restaurants in the World," which recounts his endless (and pointless) debates with friends about food—the answer is always that the best restaurants are from our own hometown, in his case, Kansas City. In my favorite passage, the one I read aloud, he describes Arthur Bryant's Barbecue (a teaching note, this works well before lunch):

> The counterman tosses a couple of pieces of bread onto the counter, grabs a half pound of beef from a pile next to him, slaps it onto the bread, brushes on some sauce in almost the same motion, and then wraps it all up in two thicknesses of butcher paper in a futile attempt to keep the customer's hand dry as he carries off his prize.

But the real treat for Trillin is the burnt edges of the brisket, which are given away for free.

> The counterman just pushes them over to the side as he slices the beef, and anyone who wants them helps himself. I dream of those burn edges. Sometimes, when I'm in some awful, over-priced restaurant in some strange town—all of my restaurant-finding techniques having failed, so that I am left to choke down something that costs seven dollars and tastes like a medium rare sponge—a blank look comes over my face: I have just realized that at that very moment someone in Kansas City is being given those burnt edges *free*. (384)

I read this aloud to my students and ask them to write about their choice for the "best restaurant in the world." I write with them and my choice is easy—Newick's, a local seafood restaurant on the Great Bay at the edge of Durham. (I am not the only one to write effusively about Newick's—my friend Tom Romano writes poetry about Newick's.) So I "borrow" Trillin's voice to write:

> Once when I crossed the Canadian border at some obscure spot, the border guard looked at my driver's license and asked where I lived in New Hampshire. "Durham," I said.

At that moment he dropped his "official" look and said dreamily, "Oh yes, Durham, Newick's."

I could tell this poor man would sit freezing his ass off in January dreaming of an overflowing plate of Newick's fried clams. And even as I write these words, "fried clams," my mouth begins to water and I think of their crispness and the taste of the batter coating.

At Newick's it's not just the food that's fried. The air is fried as well. You can smell it in the parking lot, and on a good day, when the wind is just right, you can smell it driving by on the Spaulding Turnpike. I'll crank down my window, even in winter, and take a deep breath. Inside the restaurant the smell seems almost physical, a certain weight in the air, seeping into clothes and hair. I wonder if the waitresses can truly wash it out, if they smell like fried food when they go to bed with lovers or spouses.

This is not a place for health food advocates. You can almost feel the cholesterol work its way to your heart. There is a salad you can order—a pathetic garden salad with tough-skinned tomatoes, cucumber slices and iceberg lettuce. A totally unimaginative salad—as if to say, "Why on earth would you come here for a salad?"

Strategies for Reading Aloud

In 1979, Jim Trelease self-published *The Read-Aloud Handbook*, which went on to multiple editions in multiple languages, making the case for reading aloud with all ages of children. The virtues of the practice, the strategies for reading, are so numerous that I can only scratch the surface here. But scratch I will.

- **FIND YOUR OWN FAVORITES.** One thing that we model when we read aloud is our own affection for pieces of literature. It's good to build a repertoire of set pieces you love to read. One of my favorites is from Harry Crews' essay, "The Car," where he describes the love of his young life:

  After the Buick, I owned a 1953 Mercury with three-inch lowering blocks, fender skirts, twin aerials, and custom upholstering made of rolled Naugahyde. Staring into the bathroom mirror for long periods of time, I practiced expressions to drive it with. It was that kind of car. (367)

When I read this aloud, I just love the sound of "rolled Naugahyde."

- **SCORING THE TEXT.** It's important to create and use a marking system on the text you are about to read—to remind yourself of places to pause, emphasize, lower your voice. We may not need all the vocabulary of the McGuffey Reader, but we need some. The sign of an unprepared reader is the "neutral" tone of voice, with no differentiation of emphasis. I've noticed musicians often do the same thing on the scores they use; they often cover the score with reminders or prompts to themselves ("boom," "abrupt," "agitated") that help them convey the feeling of the music. This scoring is part of the rehearsal that should precede any reading in class.

- **USE READING ALOUD TO BEGIN A CLASS.** My colleague and friend and fellow Newick's fanatic, Tom Romano, begins each class with a poem he reads. By the end of a course, students have been introduced to dozens of poems. It is a ritual that sets the tone for the class, a reminder of the importance of good writing. After a reading, the teacher and students may "point" to language that registers with them; but no detailed analysis, what Billy Collins compared to tying the poem in a chair and beating it with a hose.

- **READING ALOUD AS PART OF BOOK TALKS.** High school teacher Penny Kittle uses book talks to introduce students to books they are unfamiliar with but might want to read. These are brief, three- to four-minute presentations in which she will read a small section of the text to give the flavor of the book.

- **READ BEGINNINGS ALOUD.** As I will argue later, beginnings are so crucial to reading—which is why they are so nerve-racking for writers. So much is set in place, so many expectations and predictions elicited. A narrator is introduced, and it helps to slowly get to know that figure we will be spending so much time with. For example, what do we make of the teller in *New Yorker* writer Joseph Mitchell's essay, "Hit on the Head with a Cow"?

When I have time to kill, I sometimes go to the basement of a brownstone tenement on Fifty-ninth Street, three-quarters

of a block west of Columbus Circle, and sit on a rat-gnawed
Egyptian mummy and cut up touches with Charles Eugene
Cassell, an old Yankee for whose bitter and disorderly mind
I have great respect. (40)

This is a man in love with strangeness and eccentricity. Someone
who can enjoy a talk while seated on a "rat-gnawed Egyptian
mummy." Even as I type this description I am filled with admiration.

- **Reading aloud to highlight the reading done in a course.** At the
  end of a unit or course, I often ask students to select a short passage that mattered to them, that they would like to recall from
  the course. We go around the class and each person reads the
  passage. It is interesting and revealing what they choose.

- **Reading as a symphony of lines.** This is a variation, stolen again
  from Penny Kittle, of the previous idea. Students pick lines from
  their reading (or writing) that they find significant—everyone
  has to have one. The teacher then plays conductor, pointing to
  students who read their lines. It's a low-risk way of flooding the
  room with quotes and excerpts from the reading.

To this short list we could add a whole list of celebrations—author's teas,
readings of published authors, the reading aloud of student work in response groups, the more performed oral interpretations of poems, reader's theatre. Struggling readers will be more successful trying texts that
they have heard read aloud—so this oral reading can work as a scaffold or
an aid. And all of these practices return reading to its roots as a communal
and oral act of storytelling.

I came to the practice of reading aloud by chance, or more exactly, by
desperation. My first teaching position was in an inner-city Boston high
school, a boys' trade school that had the lowest reading levels in the city
and some of the most difficult behavior problems. At age twenty-two, I was
woefully, criminally unprepared for this teaching. Midway through the
year, there was a scheduling change that meant I would teach a freshman
class, F-9, in the always difficult period before lunch. Even the hardened
veteran teachers described this as a tough, large, unruly class. From what I
could tell, the school owned no books that could work with the group—all
I could find were old Ginn and Scott Foresman readers, too hard, too old,

too white, with those nasty double columns and vocabulary words. My experience was not the Hollywood, *To Sir, with Love* story of winning them over. Some days were chaotic beyond my worst fears.

But they loved to be read to. If the book was right. I experimented with all the urban and ethnic writers I knew—Richard Wright, Gordon Parks, Malcolm X. I found a copy of Julius Lester's rendering of Black Folktales, and must have read Stagolee a dozen times (and discovered the students loved repetition of favorites). But the true favorite, which saved my skin that year, was Claude Brown's *Manchild in the Promised Land*, a book that described a world that they recognized. It began:

> "Run!"
>> Where?
>> Oh hell! Let's get out of here!
>> "Turk! Turk! Turk! I'm shot!"
>> I could hear Turk's voice calling from a far distance, telling me not to go into the fish-and-chips joint. I heard, but I didn't understand. The only thing I knew was that I was going to die. (9)

I read that book backward and forward, some passages over and over. And often they listened, sometimes right up to the bell announcing lunch. The next year, I was able to buy some of these authors so I wouldn't be so helpless, but I kept on reading aloud, and I haven't stopped.

This chapter began with letter reading and it will end that way. One of the great gifts that Ken Burns has given this country is his recovery of letters, particularly from the Civil War. To hear them read aloud is to be connected to an expressiveness and writing skill that help us understand the immense human cost of that war—and never more poignantly than in a letter that Sullivan Ballou wrote to his wife Sarah on July 14, 1861, before he went to battle at Bull Run. He died in that battle, and the letter was found in his remains. The letter anticipates his death and expresses his love for her: "Sarah, my love for you is deathless, it seems to bind me with mighty cables that nothing but Omnipotence could break." And it ends unforgettably:

> But, O Sarah! If the dead can come back to this earth and flit un-seen around those they loved, I shall always be near you; in the gladdest days and in the darkest nights . . . always, always, and if there be a soft breeze upon your cheek, it shall be my breath, as the cool air fans your throbbing temples, it shall be my spirit passing by. Sarah do not mourn me dead; think I am gone and wait for thee, for we shall meet again.

It is writing that assures us, "I am with you." You are not alone. We hear this voice; we cannot rush over these words; we feel the writer's struggle to comfort. And it breaks your heart.

Chapter 4

Learning by Heart
Memorizing

Brush up your Shakespeare
Start quoting him now
Brush up your Shakespeare
And the women you will wow.
—From Cole Porter's *Kiss Me Kate*

As is often the case, Mark Twain gives a good picture of the mid-nineteenth-century reading practices of his childhood. Early in *The Adventures of Tom Sawyer*, there is a memorization contest in the local church, with the grand prize being an engraved, Gustave Dore Bible awarded to the first child to "get" two thousand verses by heart. Tom is not much interested in the Bible (or church), and he is a poor memorizer—though he loves the glory of winning. One boy "of German parentage" had actually won four Bibles this way:

> But the strain on his mental faculties was too great, and he
> was little better than an idiot from that day forth—a grievous
> misfortune for the school, for on great occasions, before the
> company, the Superintendent (as Tom expressed it) had always
> made this boy come out and "spread himself." (32)

But through shrewd trades of marbles and such, Tom is able to amass two thousand verses worth of tickets issued to his classmates. At a grand celebration, with the town's luminaries present, Tom is awarded his Bible. But the Superintendent insists on some "showing off" and asks Tom to display a small token of his prodigious biblical knowledge. He asks the names of the first two apostles. Tom blushes, pulls at his buttons, and finally answers, "David and Goliath." Twain mocks this practice of memorization, though to get the joke one needs at least a bit of biblical knowledge. (And in *Life on the Mississippi*, he would celebrate Captain Bixby who had memorized every bend and sandbar in the river.)

In the late-nineteenth century, as Twain was writing *Tom Sawyer*, there was a canon of "schoolroom poets"—Longfellow, Whittier, Russell, Tennyson, and later Dickinson—who were anthologized in readers like the McGuffey, read, and memorized. Later schoolroom poets like James Whitcomb Riley ("When the frost is on the pumpkin . . .") had major stage careers where they performed the poetry they had written for children. The appeal of these poets, particularly Longfellow, was so great that his bearded Godlike picture hung in many school rooms, and later many of the schools themselves would be named after him, even the building housing the Harvard Graduate School of Education. It's hard to imagine a contemporary poet who will have schools named after him or her. Many of Longfellow's poems, like "The Midnight Ride of Paul Revere," remained performance pieces well into my childhood. A colleague of mine has awkward memories of performing "Hiawatha" in seventh grade, and her teacher urging her to "throw out her chest" as she recited.

These poems were everything that later modernism rejected—they told stories, they were instantly comprehensible, they were didactic, and they rhymed. Not to mention that they were often inaccurate history. They often presented a safe, nostalgic image of America. In the analysis of American Studies scholar Angela Sorby, they were "infantilized," often written for children ("Listen my children and you shall hear . . .") and conveyed a longing to reenter childhood. We can see the same process today, I believe, with the poems of Robert Frost, where "schoolroom classics," like "Stopping by Wood on a Snowy Evening," lose all their darkness and become celebrations of New England country life.

But the recitation of these poems celebrates a form of poetry that is communal and not private, that is instantly comprehensible and not needing interpretation. It celebrates as well a connection to American history and culture, skewed (often toward a nostalgic view of New England) as it might be. It affirms a kind of citizenship, or membership in a collective "reading public." To listen to a child reciting "Casey at the Bat" is to feel part of a collective memory, a connection to baseball past. We lose, for a bit of time, the condescension that all of our more advanced education has taught us to assume. The feeling is similar to the electrifying moment on the July 4th concerts in Boston when Arthur Fiedler broke into "Stars and Stripes Forever," then turned to the audience to conduct them. Or to the sheer pleasure of singing "Sweet Caroline" along with Neil Diamond in the eighth inning at Fenway Park.

A focus on memorization was still strong, fifty years after *Tom Sawyer* was published, when my mother was a young churchgoer in Northwest Ohio. I only became aware of this late in her life. As she entered her tenth decade, her health and memory began to fail. She joked that she could just continually watch the same movie because she would forget that she had seen it. But if the conversation ever went to her early years on the family farm, her memory was suddenly exact. She could remember their first phone number. And one afternoon, she recited the opening question and answer of the Heidelberg Catechism that she memorized in preparation for membership in the Reformed Church—almost eighty years earlier:

> What is thy only comfort in life and death?
>> That I, with body and soul, both in life and death, am not my own, but belong to my faithful Saviour Jesus Christ, who with His precious blood hath fully satisfied for all my sins,

The recitation of these poems celebrates a form of poetry that is communal and not private, that is instantly comprehensible and not needing interpretation.

delivered me from all power of the devil; and so preserves me,
that without the will of my heavenly Father, not a hair shall fall
from my head. (Good, 5)

Poet Carol Muske-Dukes describes a similar tradition of memorization that she tries to instill in her students. She inherited this practice
from her mother, who early on learned big portions of Tennyson, Milton,
Wordsworth, Longfellow, and Dickinson by heart. Muske-Dukes poignantly
describes the way she would recite Robert Louis Stevenson's poem "The
Swing" ("How do you like to go up in a swing? / Up in the air so blue?"):

My mother taught me this poem as she pushed me on a swing
in our backyard in St. Paul, Minnesota. . . . She would push me
out and away from her on the "question" line (How do you like);
then I would fly back on the comment line (Up in the air so
blue). Like my young students, I was swinging within the shape
of the words; I was learning words with my body as well as my
brain; I was swinging, like them, within what would last forever—within the body of the poem, itself.

Muske-Dukes also describes her mother's ability to "quote" from poems,
to call up lines, images, aphorisms, that could apply to new situations.

This capacity for quotation would sometimes surface within my own
family. To judge from family history, there was also a tradition of learning
some Shakespeare by heart at the Tiffin Junior Home, an orphanage where
my father and uncle went to school in the 1930s. He tells the story of waiting outside a probate office in Covington, Kentucky, with my uncle after the
death of their mother. They sat and sat, waiting for assistance on a drowsy,
hot afternoon. No one seemed in any hurry to help them. After a couple
of hours, my Uncle Charles, then an alcoholic and never known as a great
student, sighed, "The law's delay, the insolence of office." At that moment,
he called to memory a phrase from Hamlet's soliloquy he had memorized,
what, fifty years earlier. And it was perfectly appropriate for that moment.

Often these set pieces were pulled from the full plays, which were not
read in their entirety; for example, McGuffey's Fifth Reader excerpts only
the ghost scene from *Hamlet*. And, particularly in the nineteenth century,
sentences were pulled for memorization and elocutionary practice—

there was, in effect, a "canon" of great sentences. These included the four-part opening stanza to *Paradise Lost* ("Of Man's disobedience . . ."). One of the most commonly excerpted lines was the opening to Byron's "Childe Harold: "Roll on, thou deep and dark blue Ocean—roll!" (Carr, Carr, and Schultz, 103). Generations of Latin students can recite the opening to Caesar's *Gallic Wars*, which was typically memorized—"Gallia est omnis divisa in partes tres, quarum unam incolunt Belgae."

By the time my mother dragged me to church, the memorization demands were modest, yet I still retain the words to the doxology, the Apostles Creed, the Twenty-third Psalm, the Beatitudes, the Lord's Prayer, and the words to numerous hymns and Christmas carols that are somehow mysteriously still there—though as kids we puzzled who "Round John Virgin" was. Added to these were the oaths we learned for Boy Scouts and Girl Scouts, and like all students today, the Pledge of Allegiance. One voluntary memorization feat, shared by many boys my age, was the theme song to Walt Disney's movie hit *Davy Crockett*, which was so popular that for the first Saturday matinee, the large theatre in our town—with a capacity of over one thousand, almost a tenth of the town population—was full. I still have the first stanza down:

> Born on a mountaintop in Tennessee, greenest state in the land
> of the free,
> Raised in the wood so's he knew ev'ry tree
> Kilt him a b'ar when he was only three
> Davy, Davy Crockett, king of the wild frontier.

Not only was this straight version memorized, sometimes all *seventeen* stanzas, but Iona and Peter Opie have catalogued the variations and parodies that instantaneously appeared in England:

> Born on a mountain top in Tennessee,
> Killed his Ma when he was only three,
> Killed his Pa when he was only four.
> And now he's looking for his brother-in-law!
> Davy, Davy Crockett,
> King of the wild frontier. (119)

One other prodigious feat of memory that I recall was that of Tom Hammond, who lived on my floor in college. He would regale us with a full recital of Robert Service's "The Cremation of Sam McGee," fourteen compelling stanzas that began and ended with one I still partially remember from his recitals:

> There are strange things done in the midnight sun
>> By the men who moil for gold
> The arctic trails have seen queer tales
>> That would make your blood run cold
> The Northern Lights have seen queer sights
>> But the queerest you'll ever see
> Was the night on the marge of Lake Lebarge
>> I cremated Sam McGee.

Great poetry? Probably not, but great fun to hear performed.

I suspect that we all carry bits and scraps (more than we consciously realize) of memorized lines—sayings, bits of hymns or song lyrics, children's rhymes, Bible verses that we may know even if we have never read the Bible ("Let he that is without sin cast the first stone"; "Do unto others as you would have them do unto you"), some Shakespeare, or a bit of Robert Frost ("Good fences make good neighbors"). And like my mother we will, most likely, retain them all our lives. But the practice of memorization, more than any others that I will deal with, seems quaint, time-wasting, part of an earlier era of bombastic recital. When I do a search for memorization, it is often connected to "rote learning," hardly a great association.

Writing and Memory

This question of memorization is part of a larger debate about the effect of print on memory itself, one that began at least 2500 years ago with Plato's dialogue, *The Phaedrus*. The last part of the dialogue is a free-form discussion of rhetoric and print, and in it Plato's primary spokesman Socrates recounts an Egyptian legend about Theuth, a god, who developed all sorts of inventions and sciences for the betterment of society—numbers, arithmetic, geometry, draughts, and dice. He was also the inventor of writing. At the court of Thamus, the king of all Egypt, Theuth presented his various inventions, and Thamus passed judgment on whether the innovation would be an asset or a liability. When it came to the invention of writing, Theuth made this pitch: "This invention, O King, will make Egyptians wiser and will improve their memories; for it is an elixir of memory and wisdom that I have discovered."

But Thamus was not convinced:

> This invention will produce forgetfulness in the minds of those
> who learn to use it, because they will not practice their memory.
> Their trust in writing, produced by external characters which
> are no part of themselves, will discourage the use of their own
> memory within them. You have invented an elixir not of memory, but of reminding. (In Bizzell and Herzberg, 165)

This is one of the first articulations of the doctrine of *technological determinism*—that changes in the communication tools we use will inevitably alter our cognition; they will make obsolete and inefficient previous forms of knowing. Thamus argues that our capacity for memory will atrophy thought, because it will be more convenient to consult the "external characters" available in print.

Socrates was, of course, wrong, profoundly wrong in his prediction. The emergence of print was not the end of memory; it placed new requirements for memory upon humans because reading is highly dependent upon prior knowledge (which is the most significant factor in reading comprehension). According to cognitive psychologist Daniel Willingham:

> The very processes that teachers care about most—critical
> thinking processes such as reasoning and problem-solving—are
> intimately intertwined with factual knowledge that is stored in
> long term memory (not just found in the environment). (22)

We need information to be internalized, to be part of our long-term memory, if it is be useful. It must be ready and not simply available in some reference book or Internet site (as useful as those are). In the words of the dialogue, this knowledge must be "possessed," part of ourselves. I began this chapter with the episode from *Tom Sawyer*, which I generally remember from when my father read it to me as a child, and I later read it to my son. My ability to write is totally dependent on the ability to make these memory scans. The only exact quote I remember was the punch line, "David and Goliath." I needed the "external" support of the text, but without the embodied memory of the passage, I wouldn't have thought to consult it.

But memorization is only a small subset of memory, and Socrates' argument may have more weight if we limited it to memorization. We are no longer illiterate societies dependent on bards to recite our epics; and fortunately in this country even the survivalists and most paranoid among us don't feel the need to memorize texts for fear that all books will be prohibited (they may be too busy stocking up on weapons). What value can there be to retaining exact verbal memories of texts that are so available to us? Augustine provides an answer:

> Whenever you read a book and come across any wonderful
> phrases which you feel stir or delight your soul, don't merely
> trust the power of your own intelligence, but force yourself to
> learn them by heart and make them familiar by meditating on
> them, so that whenever an urgent case of affliction arises, you'll
> have the remedy ready as if it were written on your mind. When
> you come to any passages that seem to you useful, make a firm
> mark against them, which may serve as lime in your memory,
> less otherwise they might fly away. (In Manguel, 63)

Like Plato (or his spokesman, Socrates), Augustine describes an interior and intimate form of knowing—which is "part of ourselves"—distinct from "intelligence," which might help us retain the general meaning, the gist. Memorization, however, allows language to be written on the mind. To "lime" your memory, according to my dictionary, is to burn the words into it. The advantage is that this language is available for comfort and guidance in times of difficulty or "affliction."

Memorization is also a pledge of allegiance, an act of loyalty and deep respect, of affiliation. As if to say that there is language so important—religiously or civically—that it must be retained verbatim. It is for that reason that oaths, pledges, and vows are regularly memorized. My wife retains the Girl Scout Oath a half-century after she learned it. And it we need a demonstration of the necessity to get the oath just right, we had one with Chief Justice Roberts' slipup in administering Barack Obama the oath of office in 2009 (to foreclose any doubt about his legitimacy, the oath was carefully re-done, exactly, after the ceremony).

Memorization is also a pledge of allegiance, an act of deep respect, or affiliation.

Clearly one text that is part of the civic religion of this country is The Gettysburg Address, which we were expected to memorize in elementary school. I could not recite it all now, but one phrase of Lincoln's is "limed" into my memory: when he describes the sacrifice of the union soldiers killed in the battle. They gave "their last full measure of devotion," an expression that still haunts me, these young men making the last willed act of their lives. This com-pact expression stirs me to imagine patriotic sacri-fice, and I think of them when I see the photographs of soldiers killed in Iraq and Afghanistan. Lincoln helps me imagine and appreciate what they have given up. Simply to retain these words is also to keep a connection to Lincoln himself and his mastery of language. It is more than remember-ing the gist of what he said, that this sacrifice was great and calls on us to live up to the ideals of the Declaration of Independence. The exact words matter, and remembering them exactly ties me to a part of history and to one of the greatest articulations of our country's goals. I'm grateful that I learned them.

I am also convinced that this isn't rote learning. It is claiming a heri-tage. It is the act of owning language, making it literally a part of our bod-ies, to be called upon decades later when it fits a situation. It is language that can stay with us to the end of our existence. A pastor in our com-munity observed that church hymns often have this enduring quality. As she sits beside parishioners who are dying, they often ask her to sing well-known hymns, and they join in the singing. Even patients suffering dementia can retain this one fiber of selfhood—and join her in singing church songs they learned in their childhood. What other learning can claim this permanence?

Adages—The People's Poetry (and Philosophy)

First, a word about sentences.

When I was a student in the 1950s and early '60s, we hardly got beyond the sentence; we learned (well, tried to learn) the grammatical parts of speech, which we encoded in complex sentence diagrams. Absolute constructions, the proper placement of participles, objective and subjective cases, the distinction of tenses, the difference between a gerund and a gerundive—this information was pivotal on any of the standardized tests in English.

But what we didn't do was actually write. And this complex analysis was likewise rarely connected to any appreciation of literature. Perhaps the rationale was the old one—that it fostered mental discipline, a form of calisthenics for the mind, a justification that can cover many sins. But progressive educators in the 1970s cited years of research that showed not only that grammar instruction did not improve writing, but that most students did not learn it well in the first place. James Moffett, the most powerful and intellectually sophisticated critic, termed these sentence pedagogies as "particle" approaches that failed to attend to the larger discourse in which the sentence was embedded. It was time, he claimed, to put the sentence "in its place" (187).

Formal approaches to literature similarly saw the literary work as an organic unit, with words and images harmonizing to create an aesthetic effect. To strip a sentence out for analysis or admiration decontextualizes it, and undermines this organic effect. This stripping also turned complex writers and thinkers—Shakespeare, Frost, Thoreau, Emerson—into single-sentence wonders, with words of uplift for T-shirts and graduation speeches. One of my college professors objected to this excerpting: "What's next?" he asked. "Great inches in art?" A former colleague of mine, Laurel Ulrich, winner of the Pulitzer Prize for *A Midwife's Tale*, is best known for one sentence from one of her earlier works—"Well behaved women seldom make history"—which can be found on bumper stickers and coffee cups and T-shirts across the country, a celebrity she fully embraces.

There hasn't always been this scholarly resistance to excerpting and quoting. For centuries, millennia actually, scholars have ransacked literature for memorable lines, sayings, aphorisms, quotations. This language takes on the role of instruction, admonition, consolation, inspiration, and wit. Indeed, there were literary forms consisting in single sentences—proverbs, maxims, *Pensées*, aphorisms. There's the story of the older man who relatively late in life went to a production of *Hamlet*, and his reaction was, "My God, it's full of quotes." An entire book of the Bible is devoted to Solomon's proverbs, hundreds of them that are meant to be taken to "heart."

> My son, do not forget my teaching, but let your heart keep my commandments; for length of days and years of life and abundant welfare will they give you. (3:1)

> My son, be attentive to my words; incline your ear to my sayings. Let them not escape your sight; keep them in your heart. For they are life to him who finds them, and healing to all his flesh. (4:20–21)

Although these proverbs are *written*, the clear intent is that they be taken to heart, memorized, so that they are present to guide action. They were to be embodied ("the Word became flesh") and not so much stored away as integrated into our worldviews. They become a frame to understand situations we face, and available when we need them. They are memorable not merely for their "wisdom," but for their artistic construction. We can recall "When the going gets tough, the tough get going" because of its reversal—the same kind of expression John F. Kennedy used in his inaugural address: "Ask not what your country can do for you; ask what you can do for your country."

Proverbs regularly employ figurative language to make concrete the moral advice they are conveying—"Make hay while the sun shines." A general principle—make good use of the opportunities you have—is connected to a specific farming activity to make it more accessible and vivid.

The biblical proverbs regularly employ this strategy for grounding abstract advice. For example:

> It is not good to eat much honey, so be sparing of complimentary words. (25:6)

> Like a dog who returns to his vomit is a fool that repeats its folly. (26:11)

Because virtually every language curriculum has an objective dealing with figurative language, the study of proverbs seems a natural way to address this goal.

Probably no one has been more fascinated with proverbs than the great Renaissance scholar Erasmus, who in 1517 published his *Adages*, a huge (and at the time a best-selling) collection of sayings from classical authors, five volumes with about a thousand sayings in each volume, many followed by short essays. This gigantic work was a testament to Erasmus' phenomenal knowledge of classical literature and his belief that the finest qualities of that literature were to be found in the widely circulated and enduring sayings, largely from the Romans. To read through this collection is to realize how Roman we still are: "break the ice," "thumbs up," "lift a finger," "no sooner said than done," "crocodile tears," "calling a spade a spade," "a rare bird," "the blind leading the blind," "clothes make the man." We can also learn that showing the middle finger as a sign of "supreme contempt" is another Roman borrowing. My father regularly told me that he had two goals for me: "I want you to be able to read and swim." He was echoing a Roman saying, inverting an insult that is found in Erasmus' adages, "He can't read or swim"—in other words, he is a real loser.

Erasmus' favorite adage was "Make haste slowly," one appropriate for this book. It is memorable because it is built on a riddlelike paradox or contradiction, like the modern "tough love" or the Taoist concept *wei wu wei*—often translated as "nonactive action." For Erasmus, this compact expression, "Make haste slowly," conveys both the need for action and deliberation. It is an example of classical wisdom and artistic compression, both of which make adages ideal for memorization, quotation, and ethical guidance.

This past is present in our own lives and those of our students, as we still swim in this sea of maxims, many of them ancient. One third grader recalled a saying that her grandmother used, "Does it look like I fell off a turnip truck?" (i.e., "Do you think I'm stupid?"). My wife remembers, "Don't cut off your nose to spite your face." This one has an interesting derivation—it comes from about 900 AD when some virgins in convents disfigured their faces, making themselves unattractive, to avoid being raped by Viking invaders.

Families also create their own lore and legends. We create expressions regularly used to motivate (and humiliate). In his wonderful memoir *Knucklehead*, Jon Scieszka tells a story of the youngest (of six) brothers, crammed together in a car:

"Move over," said Tom, elbowing Gregg.

"Get out of my space," said Gregg, kneeing Tom.

"You're squashing me," said Brian, under Jim's elbow.

"Hey," squeaked Jeff, pushed down on the floor mat. "Stop breathing my air."

"What?" said Jim.

"Stop breathing my air," came the smallest voice from somewhere under our feet.

Jim and I cracked up. "Stop breathing my air," we chanted. "Stop breathing my air. Stop breathing my air." And so, "Stop breathing my air" became a family classic.

If someone bugged you, you would warn them: Stop breathing my air.

If someone acted stupid, you could correct them: Stop breathing my air.

If you were asked a question, you could always answer: Stop breathing my air.

It still works today, a good forty years later. Why?

Stop breathing my air. (92)

In my family, there are several of these recurring sayings. As a youngest child, our son often found ways to irritate his sisters, and when they came back at him, he would quietly sing "When the wind blows, you blame it on your brother." Probably our favorite maxims came from the kindergarten teacher of our middle child Abby. In commenting on her ability to adapt,

Marge Jeffco said, "Abby is a cat and a cat always lands on her feet." Decades later, at moments of difficulty and disappointment, we have called on this saying for reassurance—"Remember Abby, you're a cat, and a cat. . . ."

I suspect that we are not unique in this treasury of sayings, punch lines, bits of moral guidance. One of my students described a family saying that was invented when she was having trouble finding things she had misplaced: "Jess, you are good looking but you're not a good looker." (Again memorable because of a poetic alteration.) Another student described an expression that his father coined when playing cards: whenever he was on a winning streak, he would say, "Feel something slipping?"—which became a standard taunt in the family. Another taunt was "You're owned" that was used whenever anyone in the family was proven wrong. Another teacher recalls fondly her father looking into the face of their German shepherd and asking, "If you're a police dog, where's your badge?" In a third-grade class where we asked students to interview parents and grandparents, one student brought in an expression that his grandfather used whenever he got out of the shower—"I sure don't look better, but I sure do smell better." Which reminded me of my own father's saying after he left the bathroom and we were waiting to go in: "It's all urine." We obviously don't work to memorize these, but by dint of repetition, aided by their poetic and metaphorical form ("Buckle up, Buttercup"), they stay in our memory and we call on them for guidance and a celebration of family. To recover and record them is to lay claim to a part of our own autobiographies.

Canonical Sentences

As I noted earlier, a practice from the nineteenth century was the memorization of "canonical sentences" or famous lines from literature like the opening to *Paradise Lost*. Among them would be the wonderful opening to Jane Austen's *Pride and Prejudice*:

> It is a truth, universally acknowledged, that a single man in possession of a good fortune, must be in want of a wife. (1)

The virtue of this practice is that the unit of memorization is fairly short and retainable. I realize that much inadvertent memorization goes on as we do repeated reading of certain books and stories—most parents who have read to their kids retain lines from favorite stories ("The night Max wore his Wolf suit and made mischief of one kind and another. . . .").

I would like to argue that we make this practice even more deliberate in our teaching so that a few great and beautiful and meaningful sentences be committed to memory. By engaging in the intimacy of memorization, we pay attention in a powerful way. We notice word choice: in the Austen sentence, the meaning would be totally different if the line read "a man in possession of a good fortune wants a wife." The "must be in want" reinforced the idea that this is a social expectation, a code of behavior, that we might expect to be violated. Memorization reminds us that individual words matter; it forces us to attend to the rhythm and construction of sentences—it is the ultimate tribute that we can pay to authors, that their words are "taken to heart."

One way to start might be with remembered lines from books that have been read to us—if students have had that experience. Students might try to recall lines, or ask parents which lines from repeated readings they recall. One of my own favorites came from the Stupids series, where the family falls asleep and awakes, thinking they are in heaven, but they look around and finally the father exclaims, "This isn't heaven. This is Cleveland."

But I would see the primary advantage being to help students retain language that captures a theme or style of a writer, to note sentences as they read a text and to return to them after the reading. They can copy out five or six short passages (copying out is another way to pay attention) and pick one for memorization. The advantage of making the unit of memorization brief, at least at first, is that it removes some of the anxiety attendant with memorizing long passages, where just getting it down, and not appreciating it, becomes the focus. Here for example is one that I mark from James Joyce's great story, "The Dead," where the main character Gabriel is contemplating his emotional failings after a Christmas party and a prediction that snow will fall across Ireland:

> Yes, the newspapers were right, snow was general all over
> Ireland. It was falling on every part of the dark central plain,

on the treeless hills, falling softly upon the Bog of Allen
and farther westward, softly falling into the dark mutinous
Shannon waves. (651)

I am always touched by the dark beauty of this ending, and the deep sadness of Gabriel as he contemplates the snow, the early death of his wife's lover, and the remains of his life.

And what a treasure (to use an old term) are these lines of Walt Whitman, his declaration of personal and artistic freedom:

From this hour I ordain myself loos'd of limites and imaginary lines.
Going where I list, my own master total and absolute,
Listening to others, considering well what they say,
Pausing, searching, receiving, contemplating,
Gently, but with undeniable will, divesting myself of the holds that
would hold me. (126)

Great lines can obviously come from more contemporary literature written for younger students. Can there be any better opening than Jerry Spinelli's beginning to *Maniac Magee*?

They say Maniac was born in a dump. They say his stomach was
a cereal box and his heart a sofa sponge.
They say he kept an eight-inch cockroach on a leash and
that rats stood guard over him while he slept.
They say if you knew he was coming and you sprinkled salt
on the ground and he ran over it, within two or three blocks he
would be as slow as everybody else.
They say. (1)

Classes can build up their own books of quotation to be memorized, performed, posted around a classroom, shared to celebrate the conclusion of commonly read books. Some can be transformed into reader's theatre—the sentences from Maniac Magee are perfect for multiple voices.

A variation on this idea is self-memorization, where students memorize passages or sentences from their own work. One of my colleagues,

Shelly Girdner, concludes her course on poetry writing by having students perform one of their own poems. She feels this expectation signals to students that their work is significant enough to be memorized, just as the classics are memorized.

The Literary Tea/Stand-Up Comedy

When I mentioned the idea of memorization as a form of slow reading to a group of local teachers, Mary Ellen Webb mentioned her literary teas, held each February, where her second and third graders performed poems. These teas are very formal events—a podium, refreshments, china, a program, and parents as an audience. I had heard about them and wanted to know about the teaching and learning that led up to these celebrations.

Students begin the year by memorizing poems as a class at a rate of two lines per day, a poem a month. At the end of the month, they perform the poem as a class as if presenting it to an audience. It is, she claims, easier and less exposing for students to learn as a group. Among the poems she uses are:

- "My Shadow" (Robert Louis Stevenson)
- "Halfway Down" (A. A. Milne)
- "Stopping by Woods on a Snowy Evening" (Robert Frost)
- "Daffodils" (William Wordsworth)

This activity fosters memory work, providing a model for how to memorize. And she calls attention to language, particularly older words and imagery. It is also preparation for students writing their own poetry. It is a group-building activity—a common experience. And it builds cultural knowledge. When I visited her class in late spring, months after this group memorization occurred, she had her third graders stand and as a group recite the poems learned in the fall, and for a brief second, I felt transported to a New England school of the previous century.

In January and February, they write their own poems and pick a poem to memorize. Mary Ellen shares a number of possibilities—contemporary children's poets (Silverstein, Prelutsky) and many nineteenth-century and early twentieth-century poets (Rossetti, Nash, Stevenson, Longfellow, Morley, Lear). She tries to connect poems with individual student interests (e.g., "Mice" by Rose Fyleman for a student interested in small animals; "Casey at the Bat" for students interested in baseball). In preparation for the Literary Tea, each student has two copies of the poem (one for school and one for home). All students, including special education students, participate. Then she has them go through three preliminary steps:

- Read aloud to a partner.

- Read to Bob—the class stuffed penguin.

- Recite the first two lines at morning meeting—the rest is done at home.

As I listened to Mary Ellen's students recite in unison, a thought occurred to me. Memorization is the great equalizer—I am convinced that whatever reading advantages adults may have, children are as good if not better at memorizing (perhaps because we become more self-conscious as we get older). In other words, we are playing to their strength.

Tomasen Carey involved her third-grade students in another form of memorization and performance—joke telling. She prepared them for this performance in several ways, first by telling a joke herself, stressing the way a joke builds often through a repetition, often of three instances (like so many fairy tales). She discussed the use of voices and pacing, creating anticipation for the punch line. Then she encourages students to find and practice jokes—and when ready to perform them at morning meeting. She had two major ground rules:

- The joke had to be appropriate for school (though she acknowledges that some kids pushed the limit). On the whole, students made good choices.

- They had to practice the joke three times with a group of students and had to get a laugh one or two times. If the joke didn't work, the group would make suggestions about delivery or wording in the joke—to help the student get ready for a presentation to the whole class. In this way, class members had "ownership" in the joke.

Students can draw from the many fine joke books for children, including *Jokelopedia: The Biggest, Best, Silliest, Dumbest Joke Book Ever* (Weizman, Blank, and Green), which has classics like:

What kind of books do skunks read?
Best-smellers.

Did you hear about the two antennae that met on a rooftop,
fell in love, and got married?
The wedding wasn't much, but the reception was amazing!

As might be expected this *sanctioned* opportunity for joke telling appealed to some students who were not the traditional "good student." Carey describes one of them—Derek, undersized, struggling reader, loner. Given the opportunity to legitimately tell jokes, he began hauling around a dictionary-sized book entitled, *A Million and One Jokes*, most of which he could not understand. But he persisted:

At first he would tell jokes that none of us got. Eventually, though he was able to work on finding a good one, practice it, and in no time Derek became one of the class' favorite joke tellers. This was his forte. This was his place to find comfort and acceptance for who he was. This gave him a real reason to read and to read for meaning. It also gave him a reason to write as he went on to write his own jokes. At morning meeting, it would be Derek that everyone wanted to tell a joke. . . . On days when nobody would volunteer, they would chant Derek's name and he would get up and do his own version of Leno's monologue, telling joke after joke. He was good.

Carey notes that this small part of her literacy program engaged students in a range of reading skills and writing skills—reading for expression, word study (multiple meanings of words), revision, audience awareness, story structure, characterization (and, of course, memorization).

A Director's Guide to Memorization

Curious about the way actors are trained to memorize lines, I decided to ask an expert. So I met with University of New Hampshire professor of theatre David Richman. I was prompted by my own attempts to memorize, which often seemed haphazard and inefficient. As I anticipated, he required his actors to engage in a much more deliberate process.

Actually, there are several steps that proceed memorization:

- The first is a number of slow read-throughs where director and actor talk about unfamiliar words, complex metaphors (common in Shakespeare), and speculate on the motives characters have for saying what they say—and construct a backstory for the action of the play.

- The second step is to add action to the lines (still not yet memorized). This allows the line to be part of what Stanislavski called "muscular memory."

- Only then does memorization start—so memorization is not "rote," as the actor has thought about the lines, teased out meanings, and made emotional and intellectual investments.

- The actor learns ten lines per day, always rehearsing the previously memorized lines. Richman mentioned that some actors like to have a prompter, others prefer to do the work alone. And even when the entire part is memorized, Richman stresses that to hold the part, the actor needs to recite his or her entire part *every day* during rehearsals and performances or it will be lost.

"No Part of Themselves"

Plato was wrong about writing—at least his prediction that print systems would spell the end of memory. Yet it is a tempting argument, particularly in this age of accessibility, when any fact or quote is instantly available through a quick Internet search. Columnist David Brooks has summarized this position (which he is skeptical of) in a column titled "The Outsourced Brain":

> The *magic* of the information age is that it allows us to know less. It provides us with external cognitive servants—silicon memory systems, collaborative online filters, consumer preference algorithms, and networked knowledge. We can burden these servants and liberate ourselves.

Human memory by contrast is an inferior storage-and-access technology. It is no great concern that over 25 percent of Americans don't know the country the United States declared independence from (some said China, a joke answer I hope). Because you can always look it up. As Nicholas Carr has written in his book *The Shallows: What the Internet Is Doing to Our Brains*: "What had long been viewed as a stimulus for personal insight and creativity [i.e., memorization] came to be seen as a barrier to imagination and then simply as a waste of mental energy" (180).

But Plato was also right if we look at his exact words: "Their trust in writing produced by external characters, which are no part of themselves, will discourage the use of their own memory within them" (165). The question becomes how do we make knowledge "part of ourselves"? The fact that we begin with print, with "external characters," does not necessarily mean that language and information cannot be internalized. Written words can be given voice, learned by heart, taken to heart, embodied, owned. They can become cellular. That is the argument of this chapter.

Written words can be given voice, learned by heart, taken to heart, embodied, owned.

As I tried out this argument with friends and colleagues, I often met with a two-part reaction. First, a form of puzzlement that anyone would be promoting such an old-fashioned idea—as if I'd turned in my progressive educator card that I had held for three decades. Then, bit by bit, the small recitations start, lines recalled from early schooling. A biology teacher calls up lines from Alfred Noyes, "The Highwayman" (also a great favorite of Anne Shirley in *Anne of Green Gables*):

> Blood-red were his spurs i' the golden noon, wine red was his velvet
>> coat,
> When they shot him down on the highway
> Down like a dog on the highway,
> And he lay in his blood on the highway, with a bunch of lace at his
>> throat.

I hear bits of Yeats, Longfellow, Dr. Seuss, and, of course, Shakespeare.

In looking up one of my favorite quotes, I came across a number of blogs that testify to the power of Shakespeare's single line from Macbeth—sleep "knits up the ravell'd sleeve of care." Here is one from a physician, "Kate," written in the middle of wrenching end-of-life decisions about her mother:

> Whenever I'd get over wrought, stressed and tired, Mom always quoted Shakespeare and told me that sleep (always), sweet sleep would "knit up the raveled sleeve of care." As a youngster and young adult I never really understood what she was saying. After many nights that turned into 36 hour plus "on call" shifts as a medical resident in training and sleepless nights with my children as infants, I began to understand.
>
> The raveled sleeve with its gorgeous pattern of continuous looping threads, damaged by the constant tugging of care in all its forms, is woven back into health by the restorative powers of precious and essential sleep. I enjoy the image, the metaphor of the raveled sleeve as life's rugged and powerful potential eats away at our serenity and balance. But sleep brings back our greatness, "as chief nourisher in life's feast."
>
> These are difficult days for my siblings and me. We face new decisions, new twists and turns, and heartache as we do our best to care for our parents. Nothing is clear; there seem to

be no good choices, just an array of options that have no guarantee of success. We do the best we can.

For now, I need to step back, accept that the sleeve of my life is severely raveled and ask sleep to work its miracle of re-weaving. ("Sleep")

This is exactly the act of memory that Augustine described, of language made physically part of us. It is language retained, embodied, and used at a moment of "affliction."

Chapter 5

MAKING A MARK
CENTERING

There is nothing particularly surprising about this way which
everyone has of deriving material for his own individual interests
from identical subject-matter. In one and the same meadow the cow
looks for grass, the dog for a hare, and the stork for a lizard.
—SENECA, *LETTERS FROM A STOIC*

For years I had to resort to a form of deception if I wanted to watch any television in my house. My three kids had favorite shows "booked," it seems through the next decade, on some list I couldn't find. If I wanted to use the television to watch a video, I'd lie and say, "It's for school." Since my kids never really knew what I did at the university, this ploy worked so long as I didn't overdo it.

So one afternoon, I settled in to watch Orson Welles' production of *Macbeth*, typical Welles (brilliant, low production values)—and on this occasion my eight-year-old son, hoping this was an action movie, watched most of it with me. Later that afternoon, he came with me to visit a friend, and I mentioned we watched the film. She asked Andy what he thought of it, and he answered: "OK, it's about these little boys who get killed."

Little boys who get killed? *Macbeth*? Where did that come from? I thought through the plot. There was one scene, a few seconds at most, where the sons of one of Macbeth's rivals were killed in their beds. It made sense that for an eight-year-old this might register more than it did with me. And if the play is about the cruelty that comes from ambition, what could be more cruel than the killing of these innocent boys in their beds? His answer suddenly made a sort of sense, though I suspect this "main idea" will never appear on a SparkNotes summary.

In this chapter, I will argue against the way reading is often represented to students as repositories, as containers of information, themes, and "main ideas." This is far too tame and submissive a version of reading to be at all appealing. And I must confess a physical aversion to the questions that regularly appear at the end of reading passages (even for book clubs); I feel as if someone else had crowded into my space. Someone else is predetermining importance, invariably in a conventional way. Someone else is doing my work. The reading passage or selection, in this way, has been contained and domesticated—standardized.

I must confess a physical aversion to the questions that regularly appear at the end of reading passages....

Instead, I side with David Bartholomae and Anthony Petrosky, who open their hugely influential college text with this declaration:

> Student readers . . . can take responsibility for determining the meaning of the text. They can work as though they are doing something other than finding ideas already there on the page and they can be guided by their own impressions and questions as they read. We are not, now, talking about hidden meanings. If such things as hidden meanings can be said to exist, they are hidden by readers' habits and prejudices (by readers' assumptions that what they read must tell them what they already know), or by readers' timidity and passivity (by their unwillingness to take responsibility to speak their minds and say what they notice). (6–7)

Comprehension, paradoxically, depends on forgetting. We foreground some ideals, claims, and facts—and background everything else. Otherwise, we might resemble a brain-damaged patient described by the Russian cognitive researcher Alexander Luria in *The Mind of a Mnemonist*. This damaged man could remember every detail of his life, but in the process was a virtual captive to the images before him—in the end, a huge disability. Much of what we read, virtually all of it, drifts into the background. We are left with "what we notice," with what strikes us as significant, central, memorable—with what Wordsworth called "spots of time." These passages give us a foothold in our reading; we make our mark (literally if we own the book) to register our decisions about significance, and we're thrown off stride with a previously marked book that carries a previous reader's decisions—though, as we will see, when readers share their decisions, the text becomes fuller and richer.

In this chapter, we will explore ways in which readers "make their mark" on a piece of reading—the art and craft of *noticing*. And we might as well start literally, with the marks we can use. Next to the unmarked page, the most ineffectual strategy is the highlighted page, those lines and lines of yellowed text. I have spent time in our library watching student use their highlighters, and sometimes it seems they are hoping that comprehension will travel up their arms, to the neck, then brain. That the mere act of running their hand over passages will have some lasting effect. Which is why a Harvard guide for research advises students to throw away the highlighter and pick up a pencil. Stephanie Harvey and Smokey Daniels offer up a useful set of symbols that they pass on to their students:

✓ = I knew that.

X = That contradicts my expectations.

★ = This is important.

? = I have a question.

?? = I am confused or puzzled.

! = This is surprising or exciting to me.

L = I learned something new. (93)

There is, of course, overlap, and after all no one is checking our annotations, but a simple system like this clearly leaves better tracks of our reading. We have something to return to when there is discussion, or when we return to the reading to write about it.

Part of the contract between writer and reader is the promise of a focus, a center—that can be both emotional and conceptual. Writing is an intentional act and the reader is responsible for being alert to the intentions of the writer. There is some effect, or set of effects or point that the writer is attempting to create. It may not be so direct and contained as a "thesis" but it is a center. As readers, we try to determine "What is this about?" Yet it is the nature of human communication that there is no one-to-one correspondence between intention and response. There is not even an exact correspondence between our own readings of the same text at different times in our lives; even if the words in the text don't change, we do.

An example: This year, I saw a wonderful production of *Death of a Salesman*, a play I had taught and seen in multiple stage and film versions. It was a play I thought I knew. But this time, I was struck by the fact that I was the same age, exactly, as Willie Loman; his sons were the same age as my children. I felt a new compassion for Willie, as he mentally expanded the traits of his two sons, how he extrapolated them, exaggerated them, and imagined glorious futures to grow from them, how he so badly wanted them to be successful. Every parent I know does this. I know I do. But this aspect of his personality had never been so evident to me before.

Finding a Center
Key Words

One of the simplest and most powerful strategies for locating a *center* in a piece of writing is highlighting what you consider key words, those that have the most explanatory or emotional weight (actually, the titles of works do some of this centering work). By now it should be clear that I am not suggesting that there is a predetermined correct answer—or even that there should be argument on this issue; in fact, the more words students pick the better, so long as they can explain why they picked them. I have tried this exercise a number of times with Jane Kenyon's poem, "Let Evening Come," which I invite you to read now and to locate a word or two that you find central to your understanding and feeling about the poem:

Let Evening Come

Let the light of late afternoon
shine through the chinks in the barn, moving
up the bales as the sun moves down.

Let the cricket take up chafing
as the woman takes up her needles
and her yarn. Let evening come.

Let dew collect on the hoe abandoned
in long grass. Let the stars appear
and the moon disclose her silver horn.

Let the fox go back in the sandy den.
Let the wind die down. Let the shed
go black inside. Let evening come.

To the bottle in the ditch, to the scoop
in the oats, to air in the lung
let evening come.

Let it come, as it will, and don't
be afraid. God does not leave us
comfortless, so let evening come.

When I have shared this poem with teachers, several words are always chosen. *Let* is selected because it gives insight into the feeling of acceptance in the poem—yes, evening will come, no matter what ("Let it come, as it will"). But to *let* it come is to be at peace with its coming—and to see this time as having its own beauty and stillness and place in the rhythm of nature.

Evening is another frequent choice, and my own initial marking. Part of my attraction is the sound of the word, calming in itself—how different the poem would have felt if *night* was used. (One teacher compared this poem to Dylan Thomas' poem "Do Not Go Gentle into That Good Night"). *Evening* is more inviting, suggesting a time of transition to night, a peaceful ending of the day. And, to be sure, there is the unmistakable connection with death—the poem was written when Kenyon was terminally ill with cancer. As I retyped this poem I mistakenly added an *s* to *lung* ("to air in the lungs"), but why does she choose the singular *lung*—if not to suggest a fragile hold on life? I had missed that in numerous readings. And *lung* appears surprisingly, ending a series:

> To the bottle in the ditch, to the scoop
>
> in the oats, to air in the lung

We would not normally see these as in any way comparable; and the sudden inclusion of *lung* seems to raise the stakes of the poem. Others in the group come up with more unexpected choices. One reader picked the word *chafing* in the second stanza, explaining that it created a tension in the poem, keeping it from being to monochromatically accepting—*chafing* is a nervous, persistent sound.

Another more predictable choice might be *comfortless*—which leads to the question of what comfort the speaker refers to, what comfort this God offers. My own reading of the poem is that at least some of this comfort comes from being surrounded by the ordinary, ongoing, even mundane details of rural life. The landscape of the poem is rich and alive—full of sunlight, animal life, farm tools, night sounds—an inventory that feels strangely supportive; the speaker is not alone or isolated but richly connected to this landscape. The poem itself is a form of comfort and consolation.

This technique of finding key words is workable for any complex text. Usually in any piece of writing, there are a handful of words central to an understanding. If I were performing this task on this chapter (what I have so far written), I would pick *central, significant, notice,* and *main idea.* Unpacking those four words or terms would take you to the core of the argument I am making. And one virtue of this kind of assignment is its utter simplicity—to find and circle one or more words that strike you as important and to be willing to say why you picked them.

Pulled Quotes

In many magazines, particularly the glossy ones, editors pull a quote or two that can orient the reader to the tone and point of the article, and these pulled quotes appear in larger print, often in a box, as an invitation to read. Selecting these quotes requires exactly the comprehension skill I am championing in this chapter. There are a number of ways that pulled quotes can be used by students. In their own writing, they can use text boxes to highlight quotes that provide a window into their writing—giving their work a very professional look. In this chapter, I might pull this quote and box it:

> *I will argue against the way reading is often represented to students as repositories, as containers of information, themes, and "main ideas." This is far too tame and submissive a version of reading to be at all appealing.*

This is not exactly a thesis; in fact, it says only what I am opposing. But it gives the spirit of my argumentative stance—that readers determine significance, that it is not entirely prepackaged for them. Students can similarly be asked to pull quotes from their reading, ones that exemplify an author's style, voice, point of view, and argumentative position. If I were, for example, to pull a quote for *Angela's Ashes* (so many great possibilities), I would pick this marvelous sentence from the beginning:

> *It was, of course, a miserable childhood: the happy childhood is hardly worth your while. Worse than the ordinary miserable childhood is the miserable Irish childhood, and worse yet is the miserable Irish Catholic childhood.*

Just as in the previous exercise, students can be asked to justify their choice—as if they had to write a short memo for an editorial meeting where quotes are chosen. This format (quote + comment) is a staple of academic writing.

To justify my choice, I would claim that in these two sentences, Frank McCourt introduces the theme of misery, but in an engaging, humorous way. The "of course" almost seems to suggest a comic detachment, as if he is saying, "Why would you even bother reading if I wasn't writing about misery?" In the second sentence, he gives an ascending scale of misery, adding a new element in each repetition—Irishness makes the misery worse, and Catholicism makes it even more miserable. Yet at the same time, this opening promises that there will be a comic sensibility that will make all this misery engaging. The book will not grind us down—and it doesn't. These pulled quotes can be copied, laminated, and used to surround a classroom with exemplary writing.

Reading Beginnings Carefully

Writers regularly speak of the terror of the blank screen and the difficulty and pressure of writing the first line or the lead. A lot is at stake, including the possibility of the reader discontinuing entirely. There's a story about a famous fiction editor who visited the writing class of an elite prep school. He explained that he had to make decisions on about twenty to thirty submissions a day, more than he could possibly read in their entirety—so he read until he had a good reason to stop, and this stopping point was often not far into the story. The students were curious about how he made these decisions so he asked a number of the students to read their own stories, and he would tell them where and if he would stop—and why. Like the old *Gong Show*, he stopped them and explained why he felt a situation was clichéd or there was a lack of tension. Not the most friendly form of teaching, but a good object lesson. Beginnings, all beginnings, matter. In his book *Blink: The Power of Thinking Without Thinking*, Malcolm Gladwell cites research that college students make up their minds about teachers in the first seconds, and these judgments strongly correlate with final evaluations.

From the standpoint of comprehension, I am convinced that reading beginnings slowly is crucial—because so many commitments are being made (which is why they can be terrifying to write). They provide conceptual information that will help us read effectively: We know from the opening of *Angela's Ashes* that McCourt will be critical of the "misery" of mid-twentieth-century Irish-Catholic society. But something more significant, less conceptual is going on—we are being taught what kind of reader we must be. Walter Ong, in his famous essay "The Writer's Audience Is Always a Fiction," claims that writers invent roles for readers, just as they invent characters and plots. Hemingway, for example, created readers who were intimate with the narrator—he would often use the definite article *the* to indicate shared knowledge, referring to "the river" (you know the one I mean). I read beginnings slowly, as they not only provide crucial information about the content, themes, and arguments (in fiction and nonfiction) but more significantly, they signal a relationship.

The same is true in movies; we naturally pay great attention to openings as they reveal conflict, theme, style: In effect, openings teach us what kind of viewer we will be. Because students are more familiar with movies, I use them to make this point, using one of my favorites, *The Graduate*. The legendary first six minutes portray Benjamin Braddock returning to his home in an affluent California community where his parents have arranged a party with his "dearest friends," actually the parents' dearest friends. Benjamin is at first reluctant to join the party but is convinced to come downstairs and meet the guests, who smother him with questions and advice (the women so want to touch him—a key detail as it turns out). The scene ends with one of these adult "friends" calling him aside to say "just one word" of advice—and that word is *plastics*, a line we all found hysterical in 1969.

So I ask students to draw a line down the middle of a piece of paper, and as I show the opening to the film, I ask them to write in the left column details they notice, to fill that side with as many *observations* as they can. After the showing, and after they have filled in that side, I ask them to write *reflections* in the right side. For example, Benjamin addresses all the guests as "sir" and "ma'am"—and this observation suggests his very formal sense of manners. At another point in the opening, as Ben walks down the stairs, the camera lingers for a few seconds on a painting of a clown—what did the director mean by doing that; was he suggesting that the guests are "clowns" in some way? The double-column approach, popularized as a "double-entry journal" by composition scholar Ann Berthoff, invites students to move continually from observation to reflection, the basic strategy of analytic thinking. It is also interesting detective work.

From there, we can move to openings of literature, which calls for the same kind of work: Take, for example, the opening paragraph of Jonathan Franzen's novel, *The Corrections*:

> The madness of an autumn prairie cold front coming through. You can feel it: something terrible is going to happen. The sun low in the sky, a minor light, a cooling star. Gust after gust of disorder. Trees restless, temperatures falling, the whole northern religion of things coming to an end. No children in the yards here. Shadows lengthen on yellowing zoysia. Red oaks and pin oaks and swamp white oaks rained acorns on houses with no mortgage. Storm windows shuddered in bedrooms. And the drone and hiccup of a clothes dryer, the nasal contention of a leaf blower, the ripening of local apples in a paper bag, the smell of gasoline with which Alfred Lambert had cleaned the paint-brush from the morning painting of the wicker love seat. (3)

I'll begin by reasserting that this opening defies speed reading. Too much is going on. Why should a coming cold front be connected to "madness," and why does the narrator feel sure that we will feel it too? Why such dread at normal details like the tree blowing in the wind? What do we make of that weird combination of details in the last sentence—sounds of a clothes dryer and the leaf blower (well that's a reasonable pair) but then the leap to "the ripening of apples in a paper bag"—are we to imagine hearing them ripen?

Even in a second reading, I felt momentarily inadequate when I came to the word *zoysia*, a word I have never seen before and had to look up (a form of grass that comes from Asia, specifically Korea). I have shared this opening with a number of experienced readers and none of them knew what it was. But wouldn't "yellowing grass" have been adequate, or even better? Why this needless precision? And do we need to know the precise names of all the pines that dropped the acorns? This excess of precision suggests obsessiveness with naming. All of which leads me, as a reader, to wonder about the mental state represented, perhaps of Albert, who seems to read disaster into what is nothing more than a coming storm. In these opening hundred words, we are thrown off balance, called to question the reliability of the perceptions of the person we might assume will be the main character—we get to play shrink and wonder if he might be suffering from some combination of paranoia, or depression, or compulsiveness. A hurried reading will miss these important cues to the story.

All writing comes to us through some "teller"; it is mediated, presented by some tour guide.

Openings are just as crucial for nonfiction. All writing comes to us through some "teller"; it is mediated, presented by some tour guide. If all aspects of personality are withheld, if the tone is purely remote and neutral, that too is a kind of performance, and not one that is very inviting or "considerate." So one of our questions, always, is what kind of guide will we have for the hours we will spend with the book? Take the masterful beginning to Michael Pollan's *In Defense of Food*, subtitled *An Eater's Manifesto*:

> Eat food. Not too much. Mostly plants.
>
> That, more or less, is the short answer to the supposedly incredibly complicated and confusing question of what we humans should eat in order to be maximally healthy.
>
> I hate to give the game away right here in the beginning of a whole book devoted to the subject, and I am tempted to complicate matters in the interest of keeping things going for a couple hundred more pages or so. I'll try to resist, but will go ahead and add a few more details to flesh out the recommendations. Like, eating a little meat isn't going to kill you, though it might be better approached as a side dish than as a main. And you're better off eating whole fresh foods rather than processed food products. That's what I mean by the recommendation to "eat food," which is not quite as simple as it sounds. (1)

When I teach this book, I ask my students to come up with adjectives to describe the writer's tone or the personality conveyed in this opening. They come up with *sarcastic* (top choice), *funny, casual,* or occasionally the more nerdy *ironic.* We then look at the language that causes them to form these judgments.

How brilliant to begin an "Eater's Manifesto" with the simplest possible sentence: "Eat food." Followed by fragments—"Not too much. Mostly plants." As if the advice, the thesis of his book, is so obvious that he doesn't even need full sentences, much less a full paragraph, to get it across. He seems to undercut the seriousness of his writing project in the third paragraph—"I hate to give the game away right here at the beginning of the whole book. . . ." The *game*? He is going to keep "things going for a couple hundred pages. . . ." *Things*? He promises to fulfill his obligation to write a full book by adding a few details to "flesh out the recommendations," a natural lead-in to his next comment on meat.

On one hand, he seems to be minimizing his own efforts—do we really need someone to advise us to eat food?—at book length. It's like he is saying, "You know it is really stupid that I have to write a whole book to tell you something so intuitively obvious, but I need to explain why something so obvious has become 'incredibly complicated and confusing.' It's really kind of insane that I even have to write it." As casual and seemingly offhanded as this opening is, Pollan deftly begins to exploit the paradox of his title, *In Defense of Food*—why does something as essential as food need defending? This is the argumentative journey he will take us on, and his opening has created a persona that I, for one, am happy to travel with.

Other texts pose more conceptual challenges. At a recent conference session on college reading, a community college teacher created a profile of the underprepared reader. Heads in the audience nodded when he asserted that this reader had a limit of about three pages for an expository text—and the topic had to be familiar and interesting. These readers give out, panic, balk (or fake it) when asked to read the more difficult longer selections of many anthologies, normal introductory reading in a typical college course. To use the current terminology, they lack stamina or perseverance. But it is a mistake to assign these general *moral* qualities to their difficulties. We are not talking about sheer doggedness and determination, though those traits are always useful. For in order to read these longer passages, the reader needs to focus both on the global intention of the piece and on the specific local facts, details, and examples. Both have to be present in the reader's mind. The reader shuttles between them—reads the facts, details, examples, in terms of the perceived intention, which gives stability and direction to the reading.

Without a general sense of direction, the reader can easily become lost in the details; there is no hook to hang the particulars on. The situation is similar to the one I feel when a Garmin is giving me driving directions (in that prim British accent). I get precise orders for each turn, and I have enough experience now to admit that this British lady knows what she is talking about, but I need a map to see the overall picture of where I am going. I feel helpless without it. All of which brings me back to beginnings. The only way readers can achieve stability in their reading, the only way they can become oriented and purposeful, is to pay careful attention to beginnings. To titles, and particularly to openings. In order to read, we must be able to anticipate; there is no comprehension without expectation. Even an expectation that turns out to be wrong is more helpful than just drifting. If we don't know how to form expectations, we are just shuttled around until we give up in frustration. We are in better shape if we anticipate. And even if our expectations and predictions turn out to be dead wrong, like the Garmin lady, we can "recalibrate."

Let's take as a case the opening to Clifford Geertz's classic anthropological essay "Deep Play: Notes on a Balinese Cockfight." It is an essay that a first-year college student might meet in any of a number of courses—anthropology, cultural studies, humanities, even a beginning writing course. Because of Geertz's literary skill, I would guess many faculty would see this as an accessible reading selection for young students—but this "ease" is illusory, the product of prior reading and habitual reading skills that the unconfident reader, the three-page reader, does not possess. The essay begins this way:

> Early in April of 1958, my wife and I arrived, malarial and diffident, in a Balinese village we intended to study. A small place, about five hundred people, and relatively remote it was its own world. We were intruders, professional ones, and the villages

> dealt with us as Balinese always seem to deal with people not
> part of their life who press themselves upon them: as though we
> were not there. For them, and to a degree to ourselves, we were
> nonpersons, specters, invisible men. (412)

There are to be sure vocabulary issues: *diffident* and *specter* are probably
not known to many young readers, though they can be guessed by context. Similarly, they will need to know that Balinese is a derivative of Bali,
an island that is part of Java in Southeast Asia.

Although the experienced reader of this kind of work will recognize
this as the traditional narrative of "arrival" in classic anthropologies, the
beginning reader will, of course, be unaware of that convention. But even
to the uninitiated, the opening can set expectations. Clearly, if Geertz and
his wife are to study this culture, they will have to cease to be "invisible";
they will need to make contact, build trust so that they might ask questions of informants. So how is this to happen? This is the orienting question that can guide a reader for the first part of the essay. It turns out that
Geertz and his wife find themselves in the crowd watching a cockfight,
which is broken up by police, and like all the spectators they run; they join
another fugitive who flees into his own courtyard; this man's wife quickly
spreads a tablecloth and brings tea, as if they had been there all afternoon;
the police come into the courtyard looking for the village chief who had
been at the cockfight, and Geertz lies, tells the policemen that they had
been there drinking all afternoon. This run-in with the police, and his willingness to lie, allows him entry to the community. He's now "visible."

The major clue is in the title, the term *deep play*, that few nonspecialist
readers would know. But even the nonspecialist can guess that whatever
deep play means, it is central to what Geertz has to say about these cock-
fights. It is a term that must stay in the reader's awareness for fully half the
essay until it is explained as an irrationally big bet, one where the bettor is
publicly placing not only a large sum on money on the line, but his status
and his manhood as well. The essay works to describe this "depth" and the
ways in which the practice of betting (with "shallower" and "deeper" bets)
orders the Balinese society.

To read like this requires what John Dewey calls "an attitude of suspended conclusion," a willingness to be uncertain for a while, to be off

balance, to operate in unfamiliar territory. One of my colleagues warns his students against "premature evaluation." The rewards of reading such texts will involve work on the part of the reader and will not result in instant gratification or comprehension. It is our job to show that there are coherent and useful strategies for making predictions that can make this work pay off.

Locating the Opposition

Several years ago, we had a required course in our graduate program that had to be taught, and I was the only one to do so. The course was a beast, "The History and Theory of Rhetoric," which covered over two millennia and dozens of intellectual traditions from Plato to Henry Louis Gates (most programs, responsibly, break this kind of course up into periods or themes). It was an act of educational malpractice to assign me this class, and it threw me into a panic during the weeks of planning. I had a spotty reading background in the area, a decent anthology with meaty excerpts and fine introductory notes, but I had to find a way to get a foothold in each of the readings without taking time I didn't have to read deeply in each tradition.

My solution was to push myself and my students to uncover who or what each of the diverse writers in the course *was arguing against*. Some idea or situation was *provoking* the writer of each piece, and if we could be specific about that dialogue, we would have the foothold we needed. I can't say this insight entirely rescued the course, but I recall with pleasure the way we dug in to describe the alternative positions in the readings, all of us unprepared but possessing a key intellectual tool, the insight that writing is dialogic. As writers, we never have the first word, or the last, only our turn in an ongoing conversation. To make a case for anything, the writer needs to be in at least two different places, needs to inhabit, if only briefly, two different positions, one to be affirmed, another to be challenged, extended, modified.

A particularly powerful form of this type of dialogue is the contrarian argument, in which the writer opens with a seemingly self-evident, widely accepted, commonsense position—for example, the general feeling that

Atticus Finch is an exemplary parent, wise, perceptive, attentive, frozen in our memories as Gregory Peck in the film. *But,* one might also argue that Finch made serious misjudgments near the end of the book, ones that nearly cost the lives of his children, when he allows them to come home from the school pageant unaccompanied; he is unable to imagine that by humiliating the Ewell family in court, that they might want to take revenge on him or his family. Which leads to the question, what in his character could have caused him to have this blind spot? And are there others—his misguided decision to want his son brought into court for the death of Tom Ewell? The sheriff talks him out of that potentially traumatic possibility. How do we explain this misjudgment? This contrarian approach pushes writers (and readers) to think beyond the obvious and commonly accepted positions, even if we cannot fully accept the alternative. We would rather be provoked than simply reassured by a repetition of the obvious.

I will reproduce below the full text of a commentary piece that I wrote on teacher stress, which follows the contrarian pattern I have described. Note how it begins with a position that I will work against throughout the piece:

Stress, Control, and the Deprofessionalizing of Teaching

Until fairly recently, psychologists accepted the commonsense view that job stress was directly related to the significance of the decisions being made. The top executive jobs, by this logic, were the most stressful because so much was riding on decisions; and the lower-level positions—the clerks, and custodial workers and receptionists—were less stressful because decisions had less impact. There was less to worry about. All this made a kind of sense.

But it was exactly wrong.

A major turning point was a longitudinal study of male employees who administered the British health system, now referred to as the Whitehall Study. Researchers were surprised to find that mortality rates and a range of stress-related illnesses were *inversely* related to job status. Top managers were less likely to suffer from high blood pressure, diabetes, heart disease—and they lived longer—than lower-status employees. The result was puzzling to the researchers since none of the employees was desperately poor, all were by definition employed, all had access to health care. One possible explanation was that lower-status employees were more likely to smoke, or have less healthy diets, but the results held even when these factors were taken into account.

So what explained the result? The researchers concluded that, contrary to popular wisdom, the lower-status workers experienced more stress precisely because they had less control over their work. In other words, those who could make significant decisions probably have a sense of their own agency and control, and this prerogative to *act* actually made their jobs less stressful than those who largely followed the direction of others.

The Whitehall results are consistent with animal studies that deal with stress and control. Animals suffer when they are in stressful environments *and have no way to affect those environments*. This powerlessness affects their autoimmune system and leads to a range of health problems: high blood pressure, the faster spread of cancer, heart trouble, ulcers, to name only a few. There is even some evidence that when animals that feel they *can* affect their environment, a Valium-like chemical is released, which helps create that feeling of resilience, very likely the sense of well-being we all get when we decide to really tackle a problem.

In the current rush to make educational decisions based on science, this evidence is significant. I realize that to speak of the psychological health of teachers, their happiness, their sense of being creative and in control of their work might seem self-indulgent (or irrelevant) to many top-down reformers, as the focus should be on student learning. But realistically, don't we all hope to be treated by professionals who are happy in their work? Do any of us want the frustrated, hurried doctor who is on the HMO stopwatch, or worse, the angry dentist?

The closer you are to ground level in U.S. schools, the more you become aware of the deprofessionalizing power of complex educational systems and programs—for spelling, math, behavior, writing evaluation, vocabulary, character education, and more. Often, especially in more affluent districts, these systems pile up on each other, creating an indigestible, incompatible mess—Christmas tree schools, with lots of ornaments. Programs for the responsive classroom, comprehension strategies, guided reading, direct instruction, leveled book, differentiated instruction, focused correction, and writing workshop jostle for the teacher's attention—all claiming to be aligned with state systems of evaluation (and all, of course, "research-based").

A key word in the advertising copy for these systems is *easy*. Check it out. There is the regular promise that by minutely directing instruction, these systems will relieve the teacher of the stress of planning and decision making, and create great results. Worried about how to introduce this lesson? Here's a script for you. As one area teacher complained, "Sometimes I think a monkey could do my work." But, as argued above, even monkeys become depressed when they lose the belief that they can affect their environment.

It is a Faustian bargain. When teachers lose control of decision making—when they prepare students for tests they have no role in designing (and often no belief in), when they must abandon units they love because there is no longer time, when they must follow the plans designed by others, when they are locked in systems of instruction and evaluation they don't create or even choose—they will not be relieved of stress. Their jobs are not made easier, they are made harder and more stressful. Some find a way to resist, but others acquiesce, though they feel, as one area teacher put it, that "the joy is being drained out of teaching."

It will surely be argued that I am too optimistic here, that only a small percentage of teachers can or will take on this creative work. That there is not time in a school day. Not enough support. It is too haphazard and unsystematic. Too slow. That it is only realistic to rely on ready-made materials, rubrics, lesson plans, and scripts that will bring focus and consistency to instruction. That teachers will appreciate the way various programs lift the burden of decision making. That instruction in subjects like reading and math is just too complex, the frameworks of assessment too elaborate, for teachers to master.

I will only point out the incredible irony of this position—that some reformers insist on high standards for students, while they have such a low estimation of teachers.

To comprehend this essay, I would argue a reader needs to get a firm sense of the position I am arguing against—those "reformers" who construct complex (and often highly lucrative) systems that take the decision-making power out of teachers' hands. These reformers would argue that these systems provide a service to teachers, helping them to manage extraordinarily complex tasks like teaching reading; they provide computerized assessment systems, lesson plans, ordered sequences of instruction, even the scripts to use in teaching. Proponents might also argue that they standardize instruction so that instruction is equalized and predictable. These systems relieve teachers of the stress of all this decision making—a great benefit for inexperienced teachers who are so numerous in many urban school systems. I argue the opposite, contrarian view: stress is *created* when humans lose a sense of their own agency.

Pivotal Moments

Before describing the activity of analyzing a critical scene in a novel or short story, I need to let off some steam about the ways in which fiction is too often turned into a watered-down form of philosophy, thus losing its human complexity, what Walker Percy calls its "proper density." From this standpoint, fiction is treated as embodying universal values, or national themes—all of which reduces it or overabstracts it. Poor Gatsby, obscured by all that talk of the American Dream, becomes an idea or ideal or worse, a "symbol"—and ceases to be the more interesting, flawed character. Close reading can bring attention back to a psychological level, to a more basic and human interpretation of behavior. It can draw on the emotional intelligence of students, their ability to read situations and motives.

One advantage of this kind of reading is that it is continuous with the kind of inferences and judgments we necessarily make in all our social interactions—we judge moods, moral character, relationships, personality based on bits and pieces of behavior. The inability to read such cues is the key characteristic of autism. This form of inferential thinking is absolutely crucial to our successful functioning, and by extension to our reading. In a controversial comparison, James Britton once equated fiction reading with gossip. Some thought this equation was demeaning to the status of literature, but his comparison made sense to me. Both fiction and gossip, after all, ask us to attend to behavior and to engage (and refine) our psychological theories and values. Who is at fault? What is he like? What does she want? Why is he doing this? What happens if I do *X*? How do they feel about each other? Where is this relationship going? We spend a good part of our lives talking (and listening to songs) about these questions. The act of reading that I am exploring here is eloquently described by Gary Lindberg in his essay, "Coming to Words":

Close reading can bring attention back to a psychological level, to a more basic and human interpretation of behavior.

> Stories and poems show us people trying to make sense of their experience—to name them, to fit them into an orderly sequence, to find language fresh and exact enough to catch what is too personal for the stock phrases. We watch both authors and characters making meanings out of what is happening to them, attributing motives to explain the odd conduct of others, and finding patterns within which their feelings count. In other words, the characters in stories are busy doing exactly what we do as readers. We are all interpreters. (144)

In making these inferences and judgments, we rely on a moral/psychological vocabulary that helps us name behavior, a set of terms that may be the most important language we possess, starting with *good* and *bad*, *right* and *wrong*; and we spend, or should spend, a lifetime refining these broad categories.

This set of adjectives provides lenses to make crucial discriminations. Much of gossip is an attempt to determine or justify the right judgmental word to apply to some human act: Wasn't that waiter actually *rude*? That dinnertime caller from the democratic committee *persistent*? That mother *overprotective*? This judgmental language can allow us to make nuanced observations—synonyms are never really synonyms. *Ungainly* is subtly different from *awkward*; *determined* is different from *driven*; *arrogant* from *egotistical*. We "make meaning" in our encounters with other people—fictional and real—by looking for patterns in behavior and making inferences in which we move from our observations to this storehouse of adjectives, a process I have already emphasized in the reading of beginnings. We are never more inferential, doing more with less, than in first impressions. Therefore, as an opening critical move, I ask students, "What term would you use to describe this character? And what causes you to choose that term? Generate several if you can."

This leads to a more extensive analysis of a scene. I believe that analysis works best with a carefully observed scene that students find crucial or pivotal. I ask students to pick a short scene that they examine as a play—as if they had to interpret and direct it line by line, visualizing it, interpreting the power relationships, motivation, and psychology of the participants. To demonstrate this process, I will illustrate it with my choice of a scene from *The Great Gatsby*, the climactic confrontation in the New York hotel, when Gatsby believes that Daisy will announce she is leaving her husband, Tom. I pick up the action midway into the scene. Gatsby has already made the claim that Daisy has loved him, not Tom, for the last four years—which Tom disputes vigorously, verging on violently, then shifting into a more patronizing tone in which he admits that Daisy gets "foolish ideas" in her head, and yes he has gone on a "spree" on occasion but has always loved her.

> Gatsby walked over and stood beside her.
>
> "Daisy, that's all over for now," he said earnestly. "It doesn't matter any more. Just tell him the truth—that you never loved him—and it's all wiped out forever."

She looked at him blindly. "Why,—how could I love him—possibly?"

"You never loved him."

She hesitated. Her eyes fell on Jordan and me with a sort of appeal, as though she realized at last what she was doing—and as though she had never, all along, intended doing anything at all. But it was done now. It was too late.

"I never loved him," she said, with perceptible reluctance.

"Not at Kapiolani?" demanded Tom suddenly.

"No."

From the ballroom beneath, muffled and suffocating chords were drifting up on hot waves of air.

"Not the day I carried you down the Punch Bowl to keep your shoes dry?" There was husky tenderness in his tone. ". . . Daisy?"

"Please don't." Her voice was cold but the rancour was gone from it. She looked at Gatsby. "There Jay," she said— but her hand as she tried to light a cigarette was trembling. Suddenly she threw the cigarette and the burning match on the carpet.

"Oh, you want too much!" she cried to Gatsby. "I love you now—isn't that enough. I can't help what's past." She began to sob helplessly. "I did love him once—but I loved you too."

Gatsby's eyes opened and closed.

"You loved me, *too*?" he repeated.

"Even that's a lie," Tom said savagely. "She didn't know you were alive. . . ." (132)

I am suggesting that we treat this passage from a perspective that Lindberg calls "naïve"; that is, as an encounter. One man tries to inform another that his wife is leaving him—and fails. We can begin by employing adjectives to describe our impression of the scene and characters in it, as many as we find appropriate. To begin, the scene itself feels *rehearsed*; Gatsby has gone over the lines with Daisy and they have agreed on all this. One can imagine him saying, "You'll tell him you never loved him and have always loved me—and that will be it. You'll never have to put up with him again." Daisy herself appears *caught, trapped*—even *frightened* as she has experienced her husband's physical abuse before. She is *malleable* and far too *weak* to stand up to the power of her husband; and she had failed to adequately imagine this scene when she made her agreement with Gatsby, as if she is responding to more powerful forces around her at the moment.

Tom is clearly the most *despicable* character in the book, but this scene shows the complex set of traits he has that allow him to be *dominating* and even to appear *affectionate* at times. He can shift from being *angry* (he "explodes" just prior to this scene, and responds "savagely" to Gatsby), to being *condescending* ("The trouble is that sometimes she gets foolish ideas in her head and doesn't know what she's doing"). And as the scene develops, he seems to show real caring for Daisy ("There was a husky tenderness in his tone"). One mark of the domestically abusive husband is this capacity for mood shifts, where shows of caring and loving are performed—and the abused partner convinces herself that this true "good" self is the real person, if only she would behave properly to make it permanent. Tom is *manipulative* in this exact way, though like the best liars, he himself may believe his own performance.

With Gatsby, Tom is *dismissive, contemptuous, superior*, as if he was not engaging a worthy opponent or rival. His money, after all, is Old Money, and Gatsby's is not. Tom instantly shows himself to be a skilled arguer, tearing down the twin positions that Gatsby tried to establish—that all this time Daisy has loved him and not Tom. He shows that this claim is simply not credible, and that Daisy must admit times of real affection (undercutting the claim she never loved Tom) and that, if she were honest, she had forgotten Gatsby, whom she thought was dead (undercutting the second part of the argument). At this point, there is nothing left to stand on; this reconstruction of the past is simply not credible even to Daisy ("Oh, you want too much").

Gatsby himself undergoes an excruciating reversal in this scene. I imagine him as *confident* when he walks over to her chair; they had gone over all this before, this "truth" that she had never loved Tom and had loved Gatsby these four years. It was all set. Daisy knew her lines (like Tom he is *manipulative* as well). But Gatsby is *stunned* by her admission that she loved him "too" during the long interval. His mental image, his fantasy, of that time is so firmly in place that he can't take in what she has said, and

he reacts physically before he can say anything at all, and then only to re-
peat what she said. The ground is cut out from underneath him. As a judge
of character, Gatsby is *unperceptive—naïve* in his belief that his story is
also Daisy's, naïve in his confidence that Tom will simply acquiesce, naïve
about the powerful hold Tom has over Daisy, naïve about her strength, or
lack of it.

Another way to approach this scene is to take a very interesting
prompt that Lindberg himself used:

> For each character involved describe what the character *could*
> say or *could* do in the scene but chooses *not* to. Explain as
> clearly as you can why the characters behave as they do. Do you
> see any unspoken rules or habits or patterns that are guiding
> them? (150)

The scene hinges on the rehearsed line—that Daisy never loved Tom.
This is how Gatsby wanted the news broken to Tom, that all the past with
him was an illusion, all now erased. But it could have happened differently: Daisy could have said something like this—"I'm in love with Jay
and I'm leaving you, Tom." If Gatsby's goal was to win Daisy away from
Tom, wouldn't this have been enough, without making any claims about
her feelings for Tom during their marriage? Was there any practical need
to construct—or reconstruct—this past? Why give such a big opening for
Tom to blow holes in? As long as Daisy was willing to go forward with him,
why is the past even relevant? The answer, I feel, is that this whole encounter is not about moving forward, but in maintaining a story that has been
in Gatsby's head since he met Daisy, one that got him through the war and
his often illegal activities making money. His meeting with Daisy was only
partly about the future, about her leaving Tom; it was just as much about
confirming a narrative, a fiction, that was deeply part of him. When he
hears from Daisy that she loved them both, this fiction is destroyed. The
book ends with the haunting image:

> So we beat on, boats against the current, borne back ceaselessly
> into the past. (180)

As much as Gatsby, in great American fashion, was able to reinvent him-self, he is defeated in his ability to remake the past.

For almost two decades, I lived across the street from Pulitzer Prize–winner and writing guru Donald Murray. When I was working on a draft of an essay or chapter, I would often give him a call to see if he would read it—and Don would invariably say, "Come on over." At first, I worried that I was interrupting *his* writing, but he said that if it was going well, he could always get back to it, and if it was going badly, he could use a break. So I would walk across Mill Pond Road, greet his wife Minnie Mae Murray, perhaps stop to admire the gigantic amaryllis that she would be growing, wend my way through the shelves of ancient canned fruit (some of it, I am sure, older than I was) and stored junk in the basement, to Don's office at the far corner. He'd be listening to a Bach cantata at full volume, so I had to be careful not to startle him as I walked in.

I would hand him my writing. He'd look at the title, and at least until I wised up later on, he'd often say, "Tom, that's not a title—that's a label." He would lift his glasses to his forehead, hold the manuscript about four inches from his eyes, read it at lightning speed, and ask me the same ques-tion, time and again—"What's this about?"

For a long time that question felt mildly insulting. "What's this about?" "Check the title," I'd want to say. Or "Maybe if you read it a little more care-fully," but I'd try to answer his question, which turned out to be harder than I thought. I'd usually have to make a couple attempts, embarrassing because it was, after all, *my* essay, and if I didn't know what it was about what chance did my readers have? When I finally offered a satisfactory answer, Don would hold the first four or five pages of the manuscript be-tween his massive fingers, "You don't get to that until page 6. You're clear-ing your throat here." And he was right, always.

It was a great object lesson for reading and writing. But not the only important lesson I received from him. A more subtle one, and somewhat contradictory one, was the need to give the reader "space." As writers we can be too insistent, too point-driven, too relentless, too guided. Texts can be too controlling. In a way, he was talking about understatement, but I think he was also acknowledging that readers will find their own entry points to a piece of writing; they will make their marks, depending on their purposes, on the associations they make, on their prior experiences, their age, gender. We reread one of our books that we marked—and wonder, why that sentence? Where was I then? The Big Lie that we present to students is that the "main idea" is already *there*, preexisting the individual reading, determined by some expert we will never meet. According to this sterile view of reading, this main idea is something we *find*; not something we *make, and remake*. A transactional view of reading acknowledges this central paradox—that writing is an intentional act and as readers we must be alert to the cues the writer gives us in titles, in opening paragraphs, in pivotal scenes, in descriptions. If we are to respond, we must be responsible. We need to be awake, to pay attention.

> *If we are to respond, we must be responsible.*

But at the same time, texts (even legal texts) are never determinative; there can never be a one-to-one relationship between intent and reception—in fact writers surely have multiple intentions, some that we are not even aware of. There is always slippage (or as Don Murray claimed, "space"); different readers find different patterns of significance, ones the writer might not have anticipated. And an eight-year-old boy who claims that *Macbeth* is about innocent young boys killed in their sleep might have something to tell us about the play.

Chapter 6

THE PLEASURES OF DIFFICULTY
PROBLEM FINDING

Error marks the place where education begins.

—MIKE ROSE

It all began in a bar—some drunk showed me a trick.

You take a regular dinner fork and spoon and wedge the bowl of the spoon into the tines of the fork so they form an arc. Then put a wooden match through the top gap in the fork tines so that you can place your index finger under the match and balance the fork/spoon (finding this balance point is a little delicate so the guy may not have been drunk after all). Then carefully place the match on the lip of a wine glass with the wood end out and lighting end inside the glass— it is surprisingly stable. You end up with a demonstration looking like Figure 6–1.

What you see violates just about everything you know about balance and gravity. All of the weight (the rest of the match and both spoon and fork) is outside the glass and *should* fall down. But they don't. If you jostle the match lightly, the fork and spoon will bob but not fall. When I make this demonstration, I ask observers to list facts they see and to use their knowledge of balance to help explain it. What follows then is interesting—an initial paralysis, confusion, perhaps unpleasant and hazy memories of science classes, a sense of inadequacy perhaps ("I was

Figure 6–1. Violation of laws of gravity, or simple bar trick?

never good at science"). Our own prior learning history comes flooding back. This initial response is a more emotional, even physical discomfort. Then, slowly, they begin to inventory what they know—what is this demonstration like? Some recall balancing positions in gymnastics. Others call up images of Philippe Petit, who walked across the Trade Towers with a long pole; others, the way we automatically shoot out our arms when we begin to lose our balance. They ask me to try it again with the arms arcing away from the glass, which I do, and the spoon/fork fall to the table. The arms bending inward, we conclude, are crucial. Someone asks me to do it again only using a light plastic cup, and I can't do it—the cup topples over, so the weight of the wine glass is crucial as a countermeasure. They wonder if the segment of the match in the glass has any effect—so I burn it off (the fire goes out when it reaches the glass—another physics question involving kindling point). Nothing happens with the balance. It remains stable with just the edge of burnt match on the lip of the glass—so that bit of wood was not significant in the balancing. I ask one of them to redo the experiment and they can feel that the wedged fork-spoon "wants" to turn, so turning or torque is probably a factor too.

We do several other experiments, and in the end we don't fully understand what we see. But we have worked through that initial period of confusion and discomfort, even inadequacy, to think about balance. I am convinced that a crucial measure of intelligence—and by extension, reading skill—is this ability to *work through* this initial discomfort of situations that don't make sense, when our habitual patterns of understanding don't do the job. Marvin Minsky, a renowned cognitive scientist, eloquently describes the attitude that I will explore in this chapter:

> Thinking is a process and if your thinking does something you
> don't want it to you should be able to say something micro-
> scopic and analytic about it, and not something enveloping and
> evaluating about yourself as a learner. The important thing in
> refining your thought is to try to depersonalize your interior;
> it may be all right to deal with other people in a vague global
> way—by having attitudes about them, but it is devastating if
> this is the way you deal with yourself. (In Bernstein, 122)

We can see the debilitating effect of "having attitude," of "global" explanations of difficulty, in the behavior of almost all reluctant or resistant students. In fact, I think we all resort to this kind of explanation at times. It can usually be reduced to the sentence ("I'm not good at _____"). A difficulty becomes an identity; and the stress of dealing with difficulties in any area (like reading) can be minimized by claiming this skill is "off-limits," simply not part of our personal makeup. So if you are not "good" at something, you have a reason for avoiding trying and publicly failing. Minsky's use of *microscopic* is also significant. When faced with a difficulty or a major challenge, an effective thinker can break apart (the root meaning of *analyze*) that problem into parts—the whole problem may be daunting, but it doesn't have to be solved all at once; it can be broken into stages that feel more manageable.

Psychologists Leslie Kamen and Martin Seligman describe this as an "explanatory style," a way of accounting for the difficulties we face. They are particularly interested in the features of "learned helplessness" that characterize individuals who feel their difficulties arise because of deep and permanent personal inadequacies. There are three key features of the explanatory style of learned helplessness:

- **INTERNAL.** Problems arise because of deficiencies in the learner and not aspects of the external situation. A student fails a test because he is "stupid." It is not due to the nature of the test—that it was hard, for example, or there wasn't enough time, or that the student didn't study the right material.

- **STABLE.** This trait is a basic part of the student's personality or competence, and not correctable by changing behavior (e.g., changing study habits).

- **GLOBAL.** The difficulty was due to a global inadequacy and not some specific, local problem ("I'm bad at math" versus "I'm not clear on the way to figure the area of a parallelogram").

Minsky claims that this explanatory style is "devastating," and psychologists have documented the strong correlation between learned helplessness and a host of health problems—including depression and even infectious diseases. The connection to school learning and reading is almost too obvious to mention. If difficulties are not depersonalized and every "big word" exposes the reader as a failure, a page of text can be a minefield. Failure hovers over everything. It is felt bodily, a sense of panic, a tightening in the stomach or the shoulders, a sense of embarrassment, maybe perspiration—I believe we have all felt it at times. It is the great enemy of learning, "unreasoning fear."

I saw this attitude firsthand in my first teaching job, in an inner-city Boston high school, serving students with the lowest reading level in the city. Many of them put on tough fronts, but when it came to learning, they were just scared kids—scared of failing in front of their peers, scared, even, of appearing to care or try. I recall vividly, now forty years later, that when I handed out some assignments, I had to be at certain students' desks immediately or they would crumple the assignment and throw it on the floor (or at a classmate), saying "This is stupid." I had never seen such a total lack of confidence. I would kneel beside their desks, reexplain, go through a few examples, and stress, "Come to me if you have any problems." It always felt like it was a delicate edge I was working on, and often the frustration was too much and they just shut down.

Psychologist Carol Dweck describes different mind-sets that help explain the limitations some learners hold to—and that some learning environments help create. She distinguishes between "fixed" mind-sets and "growth" mind-sets. The fixed mind-set sees intelligence as a capacity that you *have* to some degree and that you demonstrate through the competent performance of tasks. The drawbacks—and they are substantial—of

... a crucial measure of intelligence— and by extension, reading skill—is the ability to work through this initial discomfort of situations that don't make sense....

this mind-set is that the learner fears and avoids situations where she may demonstrate incompetence, where her "natural" talent is not sufficient to allow her to perform up to her standards. According to Dweck, "Students with a fixed mindset tend not to handle setbacks well. Because they believe that setbacks call their intelligence into question, they become discouraged or defeated when they don't succeed right away" (17). There is a heightened susceptibility to embarrassment associated with this mind-set and a corresponding desire to stay within a zone of comfort and competence.

The growth mind-set views intelligence not as something you *have* but something you *do*; it has an entirely different attitude toward difficulty, mistakes, even failure. Intelligence is not a matter of being smart—it is the capacity to view difficulty as an opportunity to stop, reassess, and employ strategies for making sense of problems. Difficulty, in other words, is not a threat to identity or ego—because, as Minsky claims, the interior is "depersonalized." One wonderful example of this mind-set is portrayed in Homer Hickam's memoir *Rocket Boys*—an account of how a group of high school students taught themselves rocketry just after the Russians launched Sputnik to set off the space race. In order to succeed, the boys had to fail—publicly. Often with much of the town watching. At the beginning, embarrassment was seemingly inevitable: fuel would be in the wrong proportion and sometimes fail to ignite, casings would split, trajectories would be off, sending rockets into their town, and early on destroying Homer's mother's picket fence. For a while, they were the joke of the town. But the boys soon developed the mind-set that each of these failures was an opportunity to refine their project. And in the end, they won a national science fair, and Homer himself went on to a career at NASA.

One reading intervention that clearly promoted this mind-set is Reading Recovery. A few years ago, I had the privilege of observing some Columbus, Ohio, teachers trained by the lead developers of the program. I remember feeling exhausted after the thirty-minute lesson; the levels of concentration by both the teacher and child were extraordinary. But I primarily came away with the sense that the program promotes a particular mind-set, a sense of confidence that whatever difficulties the children will meet, they had clearly articulated *strategies* to deal with them, ones they could name and employ. The attitude of the teacher, it seemed to me, was to convey a sense that the student was not helpless in the face of difficulty; that he had ways of dealing with the unexpected, of tackling the "big words," of monitoring his understanding. That he was smart because of what he could do, because he had a growth mind-set.

I think it is significant that Dweck describes a *mind-set* because there is more at play than knowing how to use strategies; she is describing a capacity to be in doubt, to sustain uncertainty, even at times to enjoy it. John Keats, referring to Shakespeare's capacity to inhabit so many personalities, named this attitude a "negative capability": "that is, when man is capable of being in uncertainties, Mysteries, doubts, without any irritable reaching after fact and reason." John Dewey put it this way:

> The most important factor in the training of good mental habits consists in acquiring the attitude of suspended conclusion, and in mastering the various methods of searching for new material to corroborate or refute the first suggestions that occur. To maintain the state of doubt and carry on systematic and protracted inquiry—these are the essentials of thinking. (13)

The enemy of such thinking is impatience, the "irritability" that Keats mentions, the impulse to settle things quickly. Thinking is by definition slow.

According to Dewey, this attitude of "suspended conclusion" allows space for a crucial transition in the early part of the thinking process—the movement from a "felt difficulty" to "its location and definition." When we are at the stage of "felt difficulty," I believe we are at our most vulnerable;

things aren't working, we're disappointed or frustrated, or worse, beginning to think of ourselves as "not good" at whatever we are trying to do. For example, our students seem confused and unproductive in writing groups. We may be tempted to think globally about the students ("They're just not committed to writing") or ourselves ("I'm just not good with group work"). But to name and locate the difficulty takes it outside this accusatory realm by making it specific and local. Once we make this transition, we can begin to ask: Did all the groups have trouble or am I fixating on the ones that did? Is it the makeup of the groups? Was I specific enough about what I wanted them to do? Did I give too much time so they went off-task? Even to ask these questions, to name specific causes, moves us in the right direction. Intelligence, as Dewey and Dweck define it, is not being so good you don't experience problems, but being able to reflect and deal with the inevitable challenges of a difficult profession.

On Embarrassment, Learning, and Relationships—A Digression of Sorts

Embarrassment is the great enemy of learning, but in my opinion it is too little discussed. There is often something antiseptic about the way learning difficulties are discussed, something too technical, too cold, too much like IEP language. A student might have difficulty with "blends" but that and other reading difficulties are often *felt* bodily—in the stomach, in the shoulders, in the breathing. The clammy feeling that all eyes are on us, ready to record any problem, ready to laugh. There is a physiological and emotional component to this state, one that we acknowledge every time we tell ourselves, or our children and students, to "take a deep breath" before tackling a problem. When we do this, we intuitively understand the necessity of physical calmness, composure, relaxation.

It takes extraordinary work by teachers, aides, and parents to deal with this cloud of emotion and negative feeling that can surround any problem, particularly as students move on in the educational system. To make matters worse, this student often can see some peers, maybe even their younger sisters, happily absorbed in a Harry Potter book. Reading is a race that they are losing. Teaching students how to deal with this emotional response may be the most important task we have, because no progress can be made when a body is wound so tightly, it can't proceed out of this state of self-disappointment.

So what can we do?

We need to model a process by which this emotional state is converted into something else, into something more "microscopic," more technical and defined, less self-evaluative. A student comes into my office and says, "I'm getting nowhere with this paper. I feel like I just have ideas swirling in my head. I don't have anything written, and I know the paper is due next week." My job at this point is to help the student move beyond this state of frustration, sometimes panic.

I say, "But it sounds like you have ideas about the paper, that you've thought a lot about it. That's a start." At this point, I may play interviewer. "Talk about some of the ideas that have been swirling around." I call this a "blank probe"—not exactly a question, but an invitation to talk. I may use this tactic several times. "Say more about that. Tell me more." Often I will take notes on what the student said. Once something is out there, I might summarize what I see as the two or three major ideas, and ask, "Which of these interests you?"—and invite more talk. It doesn't always work, and it rarely works if I feel in a hurry, or if I'm tired (then I do too much talking, perhaps for self-stimulation because the listening is much harder). This is slow teaching. I am modeling an act of translation, showing a way of turning a "felt" difficulty into an identified problem, a task, that can be dealt with. I am lowering the temperature.

This form of coaching depends on the willingness of the learner to be vulnerable, to admit a problem and a need for help. For many, there are cultural barriers to taking this position (the stereotypical male who won't ask for directions), as it can be seen as a sign of weakness. Self-reliance is, after all, a cherished American ideal. I am continually stunned at my own school by how many students fail to use the support systems available to them—doing badly is, for some reason, less risky than asking for help. Composition researchers Nancy Sommers and Laura Saltz have argued that a precondition for learning is the willingness to be a novice—which means the necessity of encountering problems and trusting mentors to help get them through the difficulty.

> Those freshmen who cling to old habits and formulas and who resent the uncertainty and humility of being a novice have a more difficult time adjusting to the demands of college writing. (134)

To be a novice is to trust in a system of support; it is, as Michael Polanyi argues, an act of "allegiance"—for the learner must "believe before he can know"—believe that what is being asked is reasonable and that support will be there when needed (203).

The learner who asks for help, particularly specific help, enables the teacher to become better at scaffolding instruction. No matter how carefully we model, foreground a task, provide steps and structures, we cannot anticipate the sticking points students will experience. It seems to me that as teachers we must depend on students to speak back to us and indicate where they need us—to cue us into scaffolding that they need.

It follows that scaffolding is not a purely cognitive process. Take the widely used concept drawn from the work of Lev Vygotsky—the "zone of proximal development" (ZPD). Learning, he claims, occurs in a territory when the child cannot work independently, but can be successful with the help of a more skilled mentor. At some point, the prompts, advice, and model of the mentor are internalized so that the learner can use them without assistance. It all seemed very neat and plausible. When I was taking reading courses in the 1970s, before Vygotsky's work was well known, we referred to different levels of difficulty—the independent, instructional, and frustrational. The instructional corresponded to Vygotsky's ZPD.

Yet when I started teaching it was no easy matter to "find" this zone or level, and it occurred to me that there was a problem with the spatial metaphor (zone, level)—that I was not dealing with a space (something out there) that existed, but a relationship. To be sure, the difficulty of the material was part of it, but I taught some students who seemed to *have no instructional level*. They either could do something on their own—or they were frustrated and resistant; they crossed right over to the frustrational level. It wasn't so much a matter of the material but of their distrust of me, of school, of themselves—it entailed their learning history (indeed, their history with adult white males) and previous experiences of failure. To be successful, we both, the student and I, had to *create* a zone where we could work together, where there was a relationship safe enough for the student to be comfortable, or at least not too uncomfortable, to be a novice, to be vulnerable. It took time.

Just how we work to create these relationships is, of course, a huge topic and project. In the Reading Recovery program, teachers are keenly alert to signs of progress and proficiency, often unnoticeable to the untrained eye. They reinforce what the child *can do*—so that from the very beginning the child feels competent and supported. Peter Johnston, in his marvelous book, *Choice Words*, argues that some regular forms of language use can help develop "inner control," a belief that students are *agents* in their own learning—a concept central to the Reading Recovery program. Johnston recommends that students be regularly asked, "What problems did you have today?"

> When asked as a predictable question this implies that it is normal to encounter problems. Everybody does. This, in turn, makes it normal to talk about confronting and solving problems. It also helps students identify problems and view them as places to learn, and it sets up the possibility of asking, "How did you solve that problem?" as an invitation to construct an agentive narrative. (32)

Questions like this one normalize difficulties and assume that students can employ strategies to deal with them—that they can develop a "narrative" in which they are actors, not the victims.

One thing that holds us all back from being effective at fostering this growth mind-set is the culture of the institutions in which we teach (a big generalization, I know, but bear with me). My premise is a variation of the truism that writing teachers need to write and reading teachers need to read. By extension, schools that hope to promote a growth mind-set in students need to also promote it in teachers. I firmly believe that we are all novices in something or should be. We need to be if we are to continually modify our practice.

. . . I taught some students who seemed to have no instructional level. They could either do something on their own—or they were frustrated and resistant

But something holds us back from embracing that role, from being vulnerable and open about areas where we can be better, and from seeking help. Teachers, myself included, rarely observe their peers, even though in any school there are so many models to learn from. There is excellence all around us but hidden from us by a school culture that isolates teachers. When I raise this issue, teachers and administrators often mention the difficulty of freeing teachers to do this, but any school that can create a lunch and bus schedule can surely manage to rotate a substitute teacher to enable visits. The issue isn't cost; it would be far less expensive than other forms of inservice work, and it is precisely the "embedded" and "clinical" approach to teacher education that is so highly recommended.

So what holds us back?

The answer, I feel, is self-consciousness. Observation is so connected to evaluation (and not learning) that we feel exposed when someone observes us, and the higher the stakes, the less likely we are to try something new, to be a novice, to risk public difficulty. But even low-risk situations can make us uncomfortable because the visit will expose us, reveal something that will undercut our own self-image as a professional. Here I am, an experienced teacher, a full professor for God's sake, and I have to field a set of student questions from my first-year students that indicate I was profoundly unclear in my assignment for the book review. It seems like a sea of confusion ("Should we tell the plot of the book?"). A rookie mistake, a whole series of them. I spend the first part of my class backtracking. Do I want this open to public view? (Would this ever happen to Jim Burke or Smokey Daniels?) In a more open system, I might be less self-conscious; I might see that this need for clarification happens occasionally in other classes with teachers I admire, and backing up to reexplain is not the end of the world. In other words, I could construct a more realistic view of expertise and not compare myself with the mythic Superteacher. Moreover, if I saw how others constructed and explained their assignments, I might have a better perspective on my own practice. It is great to encourage "reflection" on the part of teachers, but it is hard to see yourself when it is only yourself you can see.

In his widely distributed 2005 commencement speech at Stanford, Steve Jobs tells an instructive story about his own very public failure at Apple, a company he founded. At one point, he brought in someone to help run the company, whose goals ultimately conflicted with Jobs'. The board of directors had to make a choice, and Jobs was fired from the company he helped create:

> I was a very public failure, and I even thought about running away from the valley. But something slowly began to dawn on me—I still loved what I did. The turn of events at Apple had not changed that one bit. I had been rejected, but I was still in love. And so I decided to start all over again.
>
> I didn't see it then, but it turned out that getting fired from Apple was the best thing that could have ever happened to me. The heaviness of being successful was replaced by the lightness of being a beginner again, less sure of everything. It freed me to enter one of the most creative periods of my life.

I am convinced that what has restrained me from learning from my colleagues is exactly this "heaviness" of professionalism, this image of what I should be able to do. I am held back by a restricting vanity, egotism, fear of embarrassment, and heightened sense of self-consciousness. Some of this may be inescapably part of my psychological makeup, though I suspect that I am not alone. How much more freeing to recapture, as much as we can, "the lightness of being a beginner."

"The Scientist Must Commit His Own Crime"

In their book *The Creative Vision*, Jacob Getzels and Mihaly Csikszentmihalyi introduce the term *problem finding* to the discussion of how creative artists work. The mind-set they describe is something more than the familiar concept of *problem solving*, where the learner is presented with defined difficulty to be resolved. They argue that:

> Finding a problem, that is, functioning effectively in a discov-
> ered problem situation, may be a more important aspect of
> creative thinking and creative performance than in solving a
> problem once it has been found and formulated. (82)

The creative artists they studied actively sought out and created problems to be solved in their work. This concept is consistent with the claim of Albert Einstein and L. Infield, which they cite, that in our best thinking we "commit the crime" that we must then solve. We are on the lookout for anomalies, gaps, and situations where habit, common sense, and received wisdom are not satisfactory (or just not interesting).

A few years ago, in writing an encyclopedia of American culture entry on "Baby Boomer," I had the distinct sense of "creating my own crime," of turning what I thought was a routine search for statistics into an intriguing problem. After submitting my entry (on "Superheroes"), the editors sent around a list of topics that needed writers. We could sign up for a topic, one of which was "The Baby Boom." I wrote back saying that I was no so-cial historian, my main qualification being that I *am* a baby boomer, as I was born in 1948. They said go ahead.

One of my first steps was to obtain statistical support for the existence of the demographic bulge that came to be known as "The Baby Boom." I needed some numbers to plug in to show a pattern that we all generally understood. Namely, that during World War II, there was a drastic decline in birth rates because so many men were in uniform overseas, and that in the decade or so after the war, the birth rate "boomed" as returning soldiers began families—and that this bulge had all kinds of social and fi-nancial implications, including the omnipresence of "golden oldies" radio stations and reruns with dancers in hideous bell-bottoms and paisley. My own family fit this pattern, as my father was decommissioned in late 1945. I knew all this—except it wasn't true.

As I looked at the statistics on birthrates, I found that they were actu-ally rising during the war years to 21.5 (per thousand) in 1943, consider-ably higher than the rate in the Depression years. And the peak year after the war (1947) was somewhat higher (25.8), but not dramatically higher. By 1963, the rate was down to 21.2 and from there declined to 15.0 in 1975, which was lower than the rate during the Depression. So it appeared that rather than a "Baby Boom" there was a "Baby Bust"—that is, the boomers themselves had dramatically smaller families than their parents.

These statistics also changed my impression of the war years themselves: Many men did not serve. This was the case for two of my uncles (one a farmer and the other who ran a plumbing business), and many did not serve right away. It was only later in the war that the country was fully mobilized. Those who enlisted or were drafted could begin families before they went overseas and even father children that they might not see until the end of the war (the case of my father-in-law). As I thought about it, I had an alternative family history for these years. And the relative prosperity and stability of the war years at home may have enabled those who were on the home front to begin families that they could now support. What began as a routine search became a problem, a disruption of common sense, once I paid attention to one column of numbers. Now I had something original, and I thought interesting, to write about.

> *"How could it be otherwise?" is the central question in critical thinking.*

The process I am describing might be called "critical thinking," which everyone, of course, advocates—but it is not always clear what such thinking is critical *of*. There needs to be an object of the criticism. This object, I would argue, is routine, common sense, habit, superficiality, accepted wisdom, consensus, niceness, decorum, tradition, laziness. We "commit our own crime" when we break free of all this regulation, this dead weight, to find discrepant information, pursue anomalies, and generate alternatives—"How could it be otherwise?" is the central question in critical thinking. The great French essayist Montaigne, like Erasmus a lover of sayings, had many Latin expressions written on the ceiling beams of his study—one was *"iudicio alternante"*: altering judgment or opinion, the necessity of an active mind to keep in movement and never be fixed in one spot.

Take, for example, the maps that pull down in the front of so many classes—with north up and south down, with Europe above Africa: the United States, Canada, and Mexico above the countries of South America. That north is "up" seems a self-evident fact of nature. But if we imagine these maps as created by some cartographer up in space, there is no reason that he has to be positioned as he seems to be—on the equator with his head pointed toward Canada and his feet toward Brazil. It is totally arbitrary. Rotate him 180 degrees and we suddenly occupy the lower hemisphere, and our own country seems, uncomfortably, upside down. One might even argue that there is a bias, in our language and thinking, to consider what is higher to be better ("lofty" ideas; "don't lower yourself"), so that the conventional positioning may reinforce a cultural prejudice about the superiority of North American and European cultures. There are after all no rules (except the ones we impose on ourselves) that dictate where this mapmaker in the sky must be. All views are equally views of the Earth.

In the rest of this chapter, we will explore how problem finding is an essential aspect of slow reading—and the focus will be on poetry. But I'd like to begin with an example from my teaching of *To Kill a Mockingbird* to a group of prospective teachers. If there is a Mother Teresa Award for Absolute Perfection in American Literature, it surely must go, year after year, to Atticus Finch. To the point where I feel he ceases to be a human being at all. So one day, I posed this question to my students:

> Atticus Finch must be the most eligible bachelor in Maycomb.
> He is smart, successful, attractive, respected, and still quite
> young, in his thirties. There would also be some social pressure,
> at that time, for him to remarry so that a woman could help
> care for his children. You would think women would be throw-
> ing themselves at him. But there is no hint of romantic or sexual
> interest in the book. Why do you think that is?

This felt to almost all of my students like a transgression, an act of disrespect (though in the movie version there is a hint of a possible partner—as if the producers sensed this oddity). One asked, "What are you implying? That he's gay?" I said, "No, it's just a question that occurred to me."

A few say that we get the story from Scout's point of view, and she may not have noticed these things. I respond that Scout doesn't miss much, and is keenly interested in her father. I won't say that this spawned a great discussion; it didn't. Imagine that, these students were not keen on speculating about the sex life of adults. But it made me think that there may be some inhibition, a kind of severe rationality, in Atticus (maybe rooted in his wife's early death) that kept women away, or kept him away from them. These crimes keep us thinking, and in this case, keep Atticus human and interesting.

Another advantage to this mode of thinking—of committing crimes that we can then solve—is that we can move toward a real, authentic, reader-based structure for expository writing. As I have argued earlier, students are invariably taught to create a thesis and defend it; if this thesis is clear and well defended, the student has done the job, top marks on the rubric. But they are not taught to create any *need* for that thesis. What problem does that thesis solve? What situation does it speak to? What other thesis does it contest? If as writers they can establish this "itch to be scratched," they stand a chance of engaging readers, of inviting them to follow the pattern of their argument. They are doing real writing. There is no point in announcing a thesis before the reader is convinced of any problem to be explored. The critic Kenneth Burke once defined *literary form* as "an arousing and fulfillment of desire," surely the sexiest definition around. But *desire* is exactly what a beginning must elicit—a question needs answering, a commonly held position that needs reexamination, a tension that needs resolution, a crime that needs solution.

Looking for Trouble

One of the great contributions of the writing process movement in the 1970s and early 1980s was the way it demystified the act of writing, making it a human sequence of decisions. Writers are laborers like all other workers. The movement challenged a popular myth that creative work is a gift from the muses, a myth Linda Flower traces to Samuel Taylor Coleridge's account of the creation of "Kubla Khan." According to Coleridge, the idea for the poem came fully assembled; it did not require time-consuming choices, and because it was a "gift," it could not be repeated. Although Flower does not deny the existence of these eureka moments, she does argue that this myth breeds passivity on the part of the student, who waits by an open window for inspiration to strike. Equally mysterious "writer's blocks" strike the writer when the muses refuse to speak. I remember Don Murray scoffing at the very notion, "Ever hear of a plumber with plumber's block?"

Another form of mystification is the myth of talent. That success in writing is the result of being talented, an innate, inborn quality that you have or don't have—the opposite of the growth mind-set. Talent may be more permanent and stable than inspiration, but it is just as mysterious. What exactly is it that these "talented" people have? To believe in "talent" is again to passively accept the way the genetic cards are dealt; it is to endorse the "fixed intelligence" mind-set that Carol Dweck and others have found so limiting. But without access to the processes of composing and performing, whether it be music, public speaking, writing, art, the learner has no real alternative explanation. It is easy to imagine any difficulty you might have is due to a lack of ability, not a lack of strategies. One reason children of highly talented parents (baseball players, for example) are so often successful is that these children know that that this "skill" is the result of human processes—forms of practice and coaching, seeking high levels of challenge—that come to seem normal.

Reading, despite the huge research base and centrality in school, also suffers from mystification. The act of reading—of comprehension and appreciation—is almost completely internal. A writer at least creates an external text; a reader creates . . . a reading. From the outside, the activity of the "good reader" seems completely frictionless, automatic; the teacher comes to class prepared, thoroughly in control of the story for the day, no blemishes there. Struggling readers seem surrounded by effortless efficiency—so it is little wonder that they come to view their own difficulties as caused by some internal incapacity ("I'm just not good at reading"). I realize that Ellin Keene, Regie Routman, Kylene Beers, Jeffrey Wilhelm, Cris Tovani, and many other reading educators emphasize teacher modeling of comprehension strategies, but my sense is that students, particularly older students, still rarely see a teacher genuinely puzzled.

This is the case in my own institution. I regularly ask prospective English teachers in our program if they have ever seen one of their professors *read something for the first time.* None had. Indeed it could be argued that many would have resented a professor assigning a selection he or she had not read, and then winging through it, fumbling as we often fumble in first encounters. Our evaluation forms tell us we should come to class prepared. But preparation may be a mask hiding the very process we want students to master (reading something for the first time, right?). Our prepared certainty belies the uncertainty and possible confusion of the earlier part of our reading, and by failing to demonstrate this uncertainty and confusion, teachers can misrepresent the very process they claim to teach. If students never see skilled readers confused, never see them puzzled by a word choice, never see how an interpretation is revised in subsequent readings—it is logical for them to believe that *their* difficulty comes from a lack of reading ability.

Struggling readers seem surrounded by effortless efficiency— so it is little wonder that they come to view their own difficulties as caused by some internal incapacity.

To give an example, a few years ago I read, for the first time, *A Tale of Two Cities*, a book that, at least until fairly recently, has been a standard for high school readers. I was shocked by how puzzling the opening chapters of the book were—murky and unconnected events in England and France, page after page with no clear sense of the general direction of the plot, or even who the main characters are. I had to make a conscious effort to keep going, assuming that at some point the connections would come clear, and eventually they do. I also thought: "And they give this book to ninth graders!" It would take a pretty sturdy fourteen-year-old to manage these pages without feeling overmatched. If inexperienced readers imagine comprehension to be instant and automatic (and why shouldn't they?), how can they rationalize their own puzzlement? How can they have the confidence to see that the book, itself, created these difficulties—and that they can do something about it?

In the rest of this section, I will describe a more "transparent" way of responding, one that celebrates difficulty and puts the instructor of a first-year college writing class on the same level as students, as all in the class would be reading a poem for the first time. For five weeks, I chose a relatively recent poem with the name of the poet removed. I passed around photocopies of the poem, and asked instructor and students to mark words, phrases, lines, whatever seemed confusing or gave them difficulty. On each reading they used a different-color ink to mark the poem to help indicate the progression of the reading. After readers had resolved these confusions (or worked as hard resolving them as they wanted to), they each wrote a narrative account of their reading using their markings to cue their memory. Once the accounts were written, students and instructor shared stories of their reading.

This procedure was designed, first of all, to put instructor and student on roughly the same footing. All were reading the poem for the first time; the instructor could not meet students with a prepared reading. Second, the method suggested to the student that the reading of poems naturally involved difficulties, that it's *normal*, and that rereading the poem was a major way of working through them. Finally, I wanted to convey the message that our deepest insights come from these moment of confusion, when we are invited to do some mental work. I am not claiming that this procedure fully represents what we do in reading and appreciating poetry, but I would argue that it addresses a key block for many inexperienced readers—namely, that poetry in particular is written in a kind of *code* that is simply unavailable to them. In fact, one student expressed that view in an early response to Seamus Heaney's "Death of a Naturalist":

> If there is some hidden meaning I missed it. Just as in most of the poems we have done thus far, the author's meaning behind the poem slipped me. After I finished the first reading I went back and read again, but still there was nothing. . . . At the end of most of these poems, the depth still leaves me unknowing. I

usually look for the title for help. *I guess I haven't got a great or even good poetic mind.* (Italics added)

The imagery of this response conveys her view that the meaning of what she reads is frustratingly illusive—it is "hidden"; it "slipped" her attempts; it resides at a "depth" she can't reach. Which leads her to a classic statement of what Carol Dweck calls a "fixed" view of intelligence or in this case reading ability: "I guess I haven't got a great or even good poetic mind." Not that she lacks strategies or practice—she's just, innately, incapable. Another reader, who turned out to be one of the most perceptive readers in the class, made a similar comment:

> Admittedly, I get easily confused and frustrated. Always have and always will hate poetry. . . . My only comment is that I do not like PUZZLES, MYSTERIES, or POETRY. All are frustrating and not worth the effort.

Here again, the confusion and difficulty are represented as permanent features of poetry reading.

But as students began to unpack, some of these mysterious difficulties could be solved by simply rereading. In the case of Robert Hedin's poem "Tornado," there was an understandable misreading of the opening line:

> Four farms over it looked like a braid of black hemp

To make sense of this line, one needs to mentally insert a comma after *it*. The instructor wrote about her own confusion with the opening:

> It was not until the third reading that I finally figured out that the "four farms" *were not* "over it," but rather that the beginning was naming a location. "It" was confusing until then—was "it" the tornado—no, syntactically that didn't make sense.

Reading ahead often resolved some of these difficulties for students, as in this response to Seamus Heaney's poem, "The Death of a Naturalist":

> In reading the poem through for the first time, I got stuck in a few places—I'm not sure what "bluebottles" means or refers to.

And "jampots of jellied specks"? What jellied specks? Why would
he want them displayed at home? But then I gave up and read
on the next two lines. I realized he meant a jarful of frogspawn
he was watching hatch into tadpoles. So that section pretty
much explained itself.

Often the challenge was to make the pattern of images cohere into a pattern, which was the case with "Tornado." Students had to struggle to see
the relationship between the section of the poem that described the tornado and images of slaughter in the latter stanzas:

> of the bulls my father slaughtered every August,
> How he would pull out of the rank sea
> A pair of collapsed lungs, stomach,
> Eight bushels of gleaming rope he called intestines

In response to this section, one student commented that in his first reading
the poem made no coherent sense "except for lines in the first stanza [that]
reminded me of tornadoes I've seen and lived through in Nebraska. . . . The
rest of the poem seemed disconnected from any experience I had ever had
of tornadoes." It wasn't until his fourth reading that the poem made sense:

> My fourth time through was when it all came to light after just
> a little thinking and reflection; it dawned on me that he was
> comparing his father and the slaughter of bulls to the tornado
> and the devastating properties of retching things right out of
> the ground.

In probably my favorite response in the project, a student had worked
his way through the structure of Theodore Roethke's short poem "Moss-
Gathering," only to encounter a new issue in his third reading as he notes
a darkness to the activity in the poem, which ends with the speaker admit-
ting he "Always felt mean":

> By pulling off flesh from the living planet;
> As if I had committed, against the whole scheme of life, a desecration.

Here is what the student wrote:

> This is really far-fetched, but I get the feeling of impending
> doom as I read this. "Cemetery," "old fashioned," "underside,"
> "old," "natural order of things," "pulling off the flesh," and "went
> out" all bring to mind scenes of death and destruction? Lord, I
> don't get it. He's talking about moss-gathering, etc. Why would
> he be interested in how/why things die? . . . I don't see the con-
> nection. All of the transitions are fairly clear now so long as I
> don't get hung up on the evil words.
>   Concluding statement: What the hell is going on?

Paradoxically, this student seems closer to a deep reading of the poem
when he expresses his confusion. If he goes on to speculate about his own
excellent question, he will have something to say about the poem. He has
committed a crime he can solve.

Writing prompts like the ones in this project allow us all to drop the
masks that can inhibit learning. We can all act like the fallible, sometimes
confused readers that we truly are. We can reveal ourselves as learners, not
always the most graceful of positions.

There is a story about the very successful professional golfer, Ben
Crenshaw, who several years ago played some of the varsity golfers at his
alma mater, The University of Texas. He and his partner had just finished
a hole that both bogeyed, and the college player, perhaps not seeing a big
difference in stroke making, tentatively asked Crenshaw about the difference in their games.

Crenshaw paused, then said, "You know that bogey you just made?"

"Yeah."

"Is it still bothering you?"

"Well, yeah."

"I'm not bothered. That's a difference."

As I interpret this story, Crenshaw is not saying that he doesn't care
about the score or the errors that led to the bogey—only that he does not

react to it by being *bothered*. He experiences the problem technically—perhaps an adjustment needs to be made; perhaps the balls are carrying farther than he anticipated. But he is not carrying forward disappointment or expanding the problem into a more pervasive feeling that he may be having an off day. It is this temperament in professional athletes that I marvel at—their capacity to face failure (often very *public* failure) without losing confidence in themselves; at their ability to quickly translate a potentially emotional failure into a technical problem, drained of all negativity. I suspect those that can't do this act of translation—no matter what their skill level—don't last long as a pro.

To make this critical translation, learners at all levels need to remove their ego from this vulnerable position; we can fail without being failures. That is what processes help us do. Mike Rose, in his classic *Lives on the Boundary*, eloquently takes us into this act of making difficulty manageable, of teaching marginalized and unsure students that there are strategies that they can use to unpack the difficult texts and problems they will meet in college. As a marginalized student himself, he knew the paralysis and self-doubt school tasks elicited:

> They open their textbooks and see once again the familiar
> and impenetrable formulas and diagrams and terms that have
> stumped them for years. There is no excitement here. No ex-
> citement. Regardless of what the teacher says, this is not a new
> challenge. There is, rather, embarrassment and frustration and,
> not surprisingly, some anger at being reminded once again of
> longstanding inadequacies. No wonder so many students fi-
> nally attribute their difficulties to something inborn, organic:
> "That part of my brain just doesn't work." (31)

Rose felt this anger as an underprepared student in college, feeling "stupid to the bone," as he failed to comprehend the assigned reading. But fortunately he had a teacher, Father Albertson, who could model for him a process of understanding:

> The next day I would visit Father Albertson and tell him I was
> lost. Ask him why the stuff was so damned hard. He'd listen and
> ask me to tell him why it made me angry. I'd sputter some more,

and then he would draw me to a difficult passage, slowly opening the language up, helping me comprehend a distant, stylized
literature, taking it apart, touching it. (57)

This image of Father Albertson touching the words, reading aloud and
touching as he goes, portrays a universal and timeless act of attention.
"This is hard but important, take your time, it will, believe me, it will make
sense. Put your fingers on the words, say them aloud."

"You can do this."

Chapter 7

A WRITER'S CHOICES
READING LIKE A WRITER

I like Mozart very much—so much that I steal
from the music of Mozart. And I feel that I have
the right to steal it because I know it.

—IGOR STRAVINSKY

Third-grade teacher Jackie Jorgenson is using Donald Crews' book *Shortcut* as a text for her mentor project. Like many of Crews' books, it evokes rural childhood in the South, and in this case describes the decision of several children to take a shortcut home along the railroad tracks.

> We looked . . .
> We listened . . .
> We decided to take the shortcut home.

Jackie, as she reads the story aloud, pauses dramatically when she comes to the ellipses, and then stops to show that these three dots indicated that kind of pause. She encouraged students to use them in their writing, and soon they emerged like freckles— for example, in Jason's story about playing his beloved Xbox 360, only to be interrupted by his younger brother Calvin. Here is how the story goes:

One time I was playing my Xbox 360 and It was fun. I heard Footsteps.
  I said it was fun? Until . . . some one opened the door.
  And it was Calvin and he said I want to play! I said blah! blah! blah! blah!

Jason gets it exactly right. The ellipsis helps him dramatize the pause before Calvin came to interrupt him. To complete the story, their mother, as referee, sided with Jason, and he went back to playing:

I played and I[t] was fun but . . . I heard foot steps and It was Calvin. he was mad. The end . . . or is it.

This writer has learned a valuable tool by reading like a writer.

When I speak to writers about slow reading, they immediately claim to be part of the club. They have, all of them in some way, apprenticed themselves to writers they admire. They have learned from the language choices of these "distant mentors," and often gone through periods of imitation before incorporating these language habits into their own distinctive style. Reading—actually a specific kind of reading—is still the best writing instruction. Francine Prose, in her book *Reading Like a Writer*, describes her own slow, close reading process:

I read closely, word by word, sentence by sentence, pondering each deceptively minor decision that the writer has made. And although it's impossible to recall every source of inspiration and instruction, I can remember the novels and stories that seemed to me revelations: wells of beauty and pleasure that were also textbooks, private lessons in the art of fiction. (3)

I suspect that even the so-called "mechanics of writing"—spelling, punctuation, and usage—are learned more from reading than from worksheets or from minilessons, no matter how well timed. This chapter will add to the wonderful body of work on reading like a writer—that, in addition to Prose, includes Nancie Atwell, Katie Wood Ray, Linda Rief, Penny Kittle,

As we copy, we slow ourselves down almost to the speed at which the text was written.

Ralph Fletcher, Kylene Beers, Lucy Calkins, my colleagues Sue Wheeler and Becky Rule, and many others going back to classical accounts of imitation. I will offer both specific strategies for helping students engage in close, writerly reading; and I will also present two short case studies—one from a student, the other from a prominent literacy educator, who describe the ways in which they have been influenced by writing mentors.

A number of the practices I will explore involve some *copying*. In the Internet age of copy and paste, word-by-word transcribing must seem an outdated practice—and to be honest it was sorely misused in my school days. We often were required to write out answers "in full sentences," even if we were only inserting a word. The sentences themselves were undistinguished and seemingly endless— just one more way of turning writing into drudgery. But when we choose passages to copy, when we insert quotations in our writing, for example, we often appreciate that writing in a new way; there is some stylistic quirk, some compelling verb, some surprising use of punctuation, some rhythm or cadence that we are suddenly made aware of. There is a physical feel to how the sentence was composed. As we copy, we slow ourselves down almost to the speed at which the text was written. It may be more efficient to copy and paste, but we lose a closeness to the text we are inserting.

Much of the learning we take from our reading is tacit, and not the result of specific analysis or detailed attention; we get a feel, an intuitive understanding, of an author. My friend Ralph Fletcher has remarked that there can be too much analysis—that the most influential writers are those that "blow us away." This tacit learning is crucial. But in this chapter, I will focus on three kinds of deliberate close reading:

- **Annotation:** attending to surprising and effective authorial choices

- **Selective destruction:** degrading an effective text to appreciate skillful choices

- **Revision:** improving writing and studying the revisions of other authors

My hope is that some of these exercises will be playful, particularly as we "wreck" texts that we like. The ultimate message is that writing is the human act of making choices.

Annotation

The Great Type-Out

When Joan Didion was in high school, at about the same time she was learning to type, she would copy out some of Ernest Hemingway's stories, a practice she claims that taught her how sentences work—"very clear, direct sentences, smooth rivers, clear water over granite, no sinkholes." This is, of course, a very old technique of annotation, one that Erasmus recommended in his 1512 textbook, *On Copia*. He urged students to use "an appropriate little sign" to mark "occurrences of striking words, archaic or novel diction, brilliant flashes of style, adages, examples, and pithy remarks worth memorizing" (in Moss, 102–104).

My colleagues Rebecca Dawson and Sue Wheeler adapted this practice in an exercise they call "The Type-Out and Analysis," which can be adapted to any grade level. Dawson requires her college students to scrutinize a passage from a mentor author. Her version is demanding and perhaps more time-intensive than some students can handle, but it can be easily modified:

> Type out four pages of your mentor's writing that you like very much. It's best that it is four consecutive pages. Of course, you should have read the pages that you type out at least once through before typing them. Let the typing slow you down to notice more.
>
> 1. Mark up the selection, pointing out specifics of craft and, in the margins, explain what you have pointed out with a comment on it. Really cover the selection with your observations. Be sure that you will understand all the markings you make. Use the reading questions handout (Figure 7–1) and my model type out as a guide.
>
> 2. Then write a summary paragraph telling me what you like about the selection you chose, what you noticed in doing this type-out about your mentor's craft, and what you gained from doing the exercise.

Figure 7–1. Reading Questions

Reading Questions

- **THE OPENING:** Where does the piece start? What kind of information does the opening give? What tone does it set? Does it make you want to read on?

- **POINT OF VIEW:** From what point of view is the piece told? What is the effect of the point of view? Is the narrator trustworthy?

- **ORGANIZATION:** How is the piece organized? How does the writer make his or her point or unfold the plot?

- **COMMENTARY/REFLECTION:** How and where does the writer include commentary and reflection?

- **CHARACTER:** How is character revealed (through action, dialogue, description, commentary)?

- **DIALOGUE:** How is dialogue handled? Are quotation marks used? Does the author identify who is speaking? Does the writer describe how things are said?

- **DESCRIPTION:** What is described in detail? Are metaphors or similes used?

- **CONCLUSION:** How does the piece end? Does it end with a question or statement? Does the conclusion tie things up or leave them open-ended? Does it simplify or allow for complexity? Does it surprise or add insight? Does the conclusion satisfy?

- **SENTENCES:** What kind of sentences do there tend to be—long, short, long-long-short, varied?

- **LANGUAGE:** What type of language is used—informal, formal, flowery, plain, academic, slang, etc.?

- **TONE:** What is the tone of the piece—serious, funny, sarcastic, reverent, sad, etc.?

- **TYPE OF WORDS:** What kind of words does the writer favor—adjectives, action verbs, proper nouns? What word choices surprise and please you?

Figure 7–1. Continued

> - **VERB TENSE:** What tense is the piece in? What is the effect of this verb tense?
>
> - **PUNCTUATION:** What type of punctuation does the writer favor— commas, semicolons, dashes, exclamation points?
>
> - **TYPEFACE:** Is there much use of boldface, italics, or underlining, and capitalization for special purposes? And if so, what is the purpose or effect?
>
> - **READABILITY:** What makes you want to keep reading or not?

When I try this, I am less ambitious: I ask for a smaller section to be annotated. Another teacher in our program will isolate one or more of these writing qualities for attention (e.g., the use of dialogue). Another way of limiting it is to set a minimum number of annotations.

Color the Senses

A variation of the type-out is a classic creative writing exercise from Anne Bernays and Pamela Painter's widely used guide, *What If? Exercises for Fiction Writers*. It focuses on creating an awareness of sensory detail. Working on a photocopy of a short story or piece on creative nonfiction, the student is asked to mark the various types of sensory detail, using a different-color highlighter for each type of sense. The purpose is to help students become aware of the repertoire of detail that can be employed in writing. An ideal passage for such an exercise comes from George Orwell's essay, "Such, Such Were the Joys," a brutal account of his experience in prep school. Here Orwell describes the food and bathing facilities of his school:

> If I shut my eyes and say "school," it is of course the physical surroundings that first come back to me: the flat playing-field with its cricket pavilion and the little shed by the rifle range, the draughty dormitories, the dusty splintery passages, the square

of asphalt in front of the gymnasium, the raw-looking pinewood chapel at the back. And at almost every point some filthy detail obtrudes itself. For example, there were pewter bowls out of which we had our porridge. They had overhanging rims, and under the rims there were accumulations of sour porridge which could be flaked off in long strips. The porridge itself, too, contained more lumps, hairs, and unexplained black things than one would have thought possible, unless someone were putting them there on purpose. It was never safe to start in on that porridge without investigating it first. And there was slimy water in the plunge bath—it was twelve or fifteen feet long, the whole school was supposed to go into it every morning, and I doubt whether the water was changed all that frequently—and the always damp towels and their cheesy smell; and, on occasional visits to the local Baths, which came straight in from the beach and on which I once saw floating a human turd. And the sweaty smell of the changing-room with its greasy basins, and giving on to this, the row of filthy, dilapidated lavatories, which had no fastening of any kind on the doors, so that whenever you were sitting there someone was sure to come crashing in. (284)

What makes this passage so compelling is the way Orwell uses the "other senses," particularly smell and touch, to convey the squalid conditions of the school—and don't we react more immediately to these anyway (one of my colleagues once said he could "smell" a school that was failing). And students themselves can choose favorite passages for this exercise.

Master teacher Gretchen Bernabei employs several inventive variations on this strategy. In one, she has made up rubber stamps: one with an eye, another with an ear, another with a nose, another with a foot (i.e., movement), another with a thought bubble, and the last an empty quote bubble. Students are invited to use these stamps on their writing to illustrate how they use the various tools for building a narrative. In a variation on this technique, she simply drew these icons on sheets of paper and gave them to students in her ninth-grade class. As one volunteer read his narrative, they would hold up their sheet of paper to indicate the use of that kind of detail. (It worked!)

Tom Romano on a Mentor Text

I spent the summer of 1972 reading. I'd survived my first year teaching English and speech to high school students, and now it was summer, my first time free of work and college classes. The year had been stressful. During the months of directing school plays, it had been exhausting. I'd made no room to write. I didn't see myself as a writer, even though I harbored a dream of writing that I'd begun to feel in college when two of my short stories were published in the campus magazine. One of the books I read that summer was *Slaughterhouse-Five*, Kurt Vonnegut's fictional rendering of the Allied firebombing of Dresden, Germany.

The protagonist, Billy Pilgrim, is a gangling, inept, former night-school optometry student drafted into the army near the end of World War II. He seeks to join his regiment during the Battle of the Bulge, but is unsuccessful and wanders behind the shifting enemy lines, where he meets an American soldier named Roland Weary, a naïve, eighteen-year-old enamored of weapons and torture devices.

> Weary was as new to war as Billy. He was a replacement, too. As part of a gun crew, he had helped to fire one shot in anger—from a 57-millimeter antitank gun. The gun made a ripping sound like the opening of the zipper on the fly of God Almighty. The gun lapped up snow and vegetation with a blowtorch thirty feet long. The flame left a black arrow on the ground, showing the Germans exactly where the gun was hidden. The shot was a miss. (Vonnegut, 34)

I'd never read anything like *Slaughterhouse-Five*. Here was Vonnegut, writing in a voice unpretentious and simple (70 one-syllable words out of 87). The simile in the middle sentence I found startling and outrageous. Some of my students would have seen it as blasphemous. God had a fly? A fly with a zipper? And not just *God*, but *God Almighty*.

The contrast between *Almighty* and *zipper* seemed incongruous, yet perfect, mixing the divine with the utilitarian.

In the next sentence—with just one word, *lapped*—Vonnegut personifies the gunshot as a voracious animal. He gets me viscerally understanding the danger and power of the antitank gun, and just as I do, he reveals the stupidity and irony of the gunshot: the burnt mark in the snow showed the Germans where the soldiers were hidden. Vonnegut isn't done yet with craft and meaning. He teaches me about *payoff*, about ending a paragraph with a final reward for the reader. The last sentence of only five words adds one more irony and shows the soldiers' futility: "The shot was a miss."

You could write like this? With blunt information and common nouns? With brevity, clarity, and unadorned declarative sentences? With written language that read like surprising conversation? With humor and implicit irony? Yes, you could.

Wrecking a Text

One excellent way of appreciating style is to fracture or modify a classic. In his TV series on the performance of classical music, *Keeping Score*, Michael Tilson Thomas does this with Shostakovich's Fifth Symphony, which was composed in the most harrowing circumstances. The year was 1937, a time of purges in the Soviet Union. The composer had been sharply criticized by the Kremlin, surely under Stalin's orders, for his opera, *Lady Macbeth of the Mtsensk District*, which official newspapers called unmusical and immoral. For a time, he awaited the dreaded nighttime knock on the door and limousine ride to Lubyanka Prison that ended the lives of many out-of-favor artists and intellectuals. A similar reaction to his Fifth Symphony would surely mean the end.

The question Thomas addresses is whether the last resounding movement of the symphony was an accommodation to Stalin, fitting a triumphal style appropriate for Soviet music—or whether it was something else. Thomas demonstrates that if Shostakovich truly wanted it to be triumphal, he could have composed it differently—and he played a subtly different and less discordant version (it all came down to one note). Then he played Shostakovich's score, which had a dark undercurrent, suggesting something less than full-hearted endorsement of Soviet-style music (the composer later said that he wanted the ending to feel "forced, created under threat"). This *teaching by contrast* can also serve us well in reading carefully for style. It was a technique used by Samuel Taylor Coleridge's ferocious and dynamic teacher, the Reverend James Bowyer:

> I well remember that, availing himself of the synonymes to the Homer of Didymus, he made us attempt to show, with regard to each, why it would not have answered the same purpose; and wherein consisted the peculiar fitness of the word in the original text. (In Brower, 7)

Wrecking highlights the choices that authors make; it disrupts the seeming inevitability of the language. And it can be displayed in read-alouds where the teacher raises a question about the author's choices, as was the case in a third-grade classroom I visited. The teacher chose Roald Dahl's *Fantastic Mr. Fox* ("I'm going to show you what is going on in the mystery of Mrs. Wisniewski's brain"). She selected the chapter where Mr. Fox and his band of young foxes are tunneling into a chicken shed. The foxes finally reach the floorboards of the shed, push them up, and enter:

> "I've done it!" he yelled. "I've done it the first time! I've done it. I've done it." [I'm thinking Mr. Fox thinks he's pretty clever— that's what was going through my mind.]

The most interesting moment in the read-aloud occurred when Mr. Fox kills the chickens:

> Then Mr. Fox chose three of the plumpest hens, and with a clever flick of his jaws he killed them instantly. ["Killed them instantly." I'm thinking the author did that pretty quickly. "Killed them instantly." He doesn't talk about it. Why so quickly? He doesn't even say he bites into them. There are no feathers, no blood."]

Adam raises his hand and comments, "It's not really a killing book." And Mrs. Wisniewski agrees that "Most children's books don't show blood."

I thought this was a subtle and effective lesson in word choice, *flick of the jaws* rather than *bite*. *Bite* may not wreck the text, but it makes it more violent and realistic; it would make Mr. Fox vicious in a way that would not be in tune with the story. An excellent craft lesson.

Cloze Procedure

One relatively simple way to employ this technique is to borrow a technique sometimes used in reading instruction where a word is left blank and the reader, using her intuitive knowledge of context and syntax, guesses the missing word. Good readers are surprisingly adept at making these guesses and maintaining the gist of the sentence. But they cannot predict the inventive choices of a skilled stylist like the writer William Nolte in this sentence describing H. L. Mencken:

> He wrote with a _____ indifference to feelings. (In Trimble, 66)

So what would we pick? Probably something to intensify or stress just how indifferent he was—so perhaps *extreme*, or *utter*, or *complete*, all conventional choices that make sense. But here is the way the sentence reads:

> He wrote with a surgical indifference to feelings.

In other words, he had elevated indifference to an art form—a great description of Mencken.

Students can be asked to create their own cloze exercises to highlight a great choice of words by an author they admire. Here would be my choice, from Emily Dickinson's well-known poem, "A Narrow Fellow in the Grass," where she describes a moment of panic when she sees a snake:

> But never met this Fellow
> Attended, or alone
> Without a tighter breathing
> And _____ at the Bone—

It's difficult to imagine feelings "at the Bone," but *numbness* might work, that paralyzed feeling of panic. But the word is, of course, *Zero*—a magical choice, a number (if zero can be said to be a number) that makes us think of this paralysis in a new way. It helps the reader imagine the blankness of the moment, as if your interior, or at least your bone structure, is empty for a moment.

Rebecca Dawson extends this contrastive practice in an exercise she calls "wrecking a text"—transforming a passage you admire into ordinary language in order to attend consciously to craft. Here are her directions:

1. Type out two pages of your mentor's writing that you admire.

2. Then retype it and wreck it. For example, make the fresh writing dull, flatten the active verbs, make specifics general, turn interesting similes and metaphors into clichés, tell instead of show, make the word choice less interesting, summarize dialogue and scenes.

3. Write a paragraph, explaining what you realized about your mentor's writing from doing this.

Many of her students describe the sacrilegious pleasure they felt in degrading the prose of admired writers—but they pay attention to style in a new way. Here is what one of her students wrote about Bill Bryson:

> Wrecking this text meant taking out all the good stuff so it caused me to think about what it is in Bryson's writing that is so good. . . . [One example] of Bryson's technique of showing and not just telling appears when he describes the William Faulkner Museum. "It must be unnerving to be so famous that you know they are going to come in the moment you croak and hang velvet cords across all the doorways and treat everything with reverence." The image of the velvet cords across the doorways makes it much better writing than saying, "They will make your house into a museum" because I got a picture in my mind of someone putting velvet across my doorway.

For my own wrecking act, I chose the opening to Dagoberto Gilb's short essay, "Victoria." It is an account of his work in construction in Los Angeles, during a miserably hot summer. The *Victoria* of the title is Victoria Principal, the impossibly beautiful actress on the hit show *Dallas*, then in reruns—and in this miserable summer he meets her, improbably, as she is waiting for her limo near one of Gilb's construction sites:

> Victoria Principal of *Dallas*. She sat down a yard from me.
> Maybe less when I think about. Yes, less. Expert with a carpen-
> ter's tape, I assure you, reconsidering it now, it was less. Her pre-
> cious hips were between sixteen and twenty inches from mine
> when she sat down. (109)

It is the opening of the essay that I chose to wreck:

> I'll even blame the heat for my inability to remember which
> year it was—1986, give or take. It was hot like never before, my
> skin so porous it was hard to distinguish which side of it I was
> on. Like I would sweat and become a puddle. A dirty puddle,
> because I'd absorbed the construction site. And because this
> was Los Angeles, and it was smoggy too. But you know what, it
> wasn't the smog or the dirt or the cement dust, it was the heat
> that seemed to drain all the color into an overexposed gauze.
> It was so hot. I'm talking about three digits, so don't think I'm
> exaggerating. It was so hot. It was so hot everybody had to say it
> again and again. So hot I don't remember if the heat lasted three
> weeks, a month, two, three. It was day and night hot, as forever
> and endless as boredom. (105)

With apologies to Gilb, here is my version:

> It was so hot I don't remember what year it was, maybe 1986. It
> was so hot I felt like I would melt into a puddle of sweat—dirty
> sweat because I was working construction. And because I was
> working in Los Angeles the smog made it worse. But really, it
> wasn't the smog or cement dust that made it bad—it was the
> heat. It was in the hundreds, and people couldn't talk about
> anything else. I don't even remember how long it lasted, three
> weeks, a month, more—it seemed endless.

The main quality that my version loses is, of course, the loose, inventive free association of the speaker. Gilb's version begins as if we are in mid-conversation. His own language seems to propel him forward ("become a puddle. A dirty puddle . . ."), a quality that my version washed away. In my version, I say that people kept talking about the heat, but Gilb shows that through the repetitions ("It was hot. It was so hot . . ."). Lost also are the rich metaphoric comparisons—"overexposed gauze," "absorbed the construction site," "endless as boredom," and my personal favorite, "my skin so porous I didn't know which side I was on." These expressions form an interesting mix with a colloquial tone of the description. One might generously say that I conveyed some of the basic information, but I stripped the passage of energetic intensity of the language that made it worth reading.

> *Wrecking highlights the choices that authors make; it disrupts the seeming inevitability of the language.*

Wrecking Punctuation

For many students punctuation is a trap; the more marks they try to use, the greater the possibility of error. So the best, defensive strategy is to play it safe with periods and commas, sprinkled lightly. The more interesting marks—the colon, semicolon, dash, and parentheses—are avoided, even though they enable the writer to embed, comment, extend, and qualify. A healthier strategy is to teach punctuation, not as a rule-bound practice but as an interesting set of tools. This contrastive, "wrecking" approach can help students see what these marks can do. So I have asked students

- to pick a favorite author and find a place where he or she uses a punctuation mark (particularly the four that students avoid) in an effective way

- to copy out that sentence

- to rewrite the sentence without that mark, in a more conventional way

- and finally, to comment on what is gained by the author's use of that mark

I chose for my own example what has to be the greatest use of parentheses in all literature, from the opening to Vladimir Nabokov's *Lolita*:

> My very photogenic mother died in a freak accident (picnic, lightning) when I was three, and save for a pocket of warmth in the darkest past, nothing of her exists within the hollows and dells of memory. (12)

What kind of narrator, or human being, would so minimize the circumstances of his own mother's death, to put them in parentheses, and not even a full statement in the parentheses? My wrecked version would look like this:

> My very photogenic mother died in a freak accident when I was three. She was struck by lightning at a picnic. Save for . . .

or

> My very photogenic mother died in a freak accident when I was three—struck by lightning at a picnic. Save for . . .

I have preserved all of the information, but have lost the wicked, amoral humor that we come to expect from the narrator. My version loses this sense of personality that the parenthetical marks give. When I use the dash, I convey just the opposite of the understatement that the original conveys; I make her death conventionally significant, but for the author it is an aside.

Helene Kenney on a Mentor Text

From *The House on Mango Street* by Sandra Cisneros

Sally, do you sometimes wish you didn't have to go home? Do you wish your feet would one day keep walking and take you far away from Mango Street, far away and maybe your feet would stop in front of a house, a nice one with flowers and big windows and steps for you to climb up two by two upstairs to where a room is waiting for you. And if you opened the little window latch and gave it a shove, the windows would swing open, all the sky would come in. There'd be no nosy neighbors watching, no motorcycles and cars, no sheets and towels and laundry. Only trees and more trees and plenty of blue sky. And you could laugh, Sally. You could go to sleep and wake up and never have to think who likes and doesn't like you. You could close your eyes and you wouldn't have to worry what people said because you never belonged here anyway and nobody could make you sad and nobody would think you're strange because you like to dream and dream. (82–83)

To make your readers think requires passion. Throughout the entire time I read *The House on Mango Street*, I found myself thinking a lot. Not about how the weather was today, or of a current predicament with a math project, but of what Sandra Cisneros really meant when she wrote this, or what she really meant  when she wrote that. Then I read this passage, and I was struck by how real she can make her writing. "You could close your eyes and you wouldn't have to worry what people said because you never belonged here anyway and nobody could make you sad and nobody would think you're strange because you like to dream and dream."

Notice. Simplicity in itself holds its own kind of elegance. Can you almost hear the words coming out of this girl's mouth? Can you hear the beauty in these words that she creates for a girl that she pities? Can you sense the pain that Sally is feeling, in a world that no one belongs in? Can you hear the truth in these words? Can you?

"And if you opened the little window latch and gave it a shove, the windows would swing open, all the sky would come in." Notice. She doesn't waste her time with big words, or predictability, but she can make this little girl real, with none of those things. More real than the heroes, the villains, the love triangles, and the action scenes. Just a little girl with wishes. And what Sandra Cisneros does with this character isn't just powerful. It's magical.

Revision

Not So Fast—A Last Editing Check

I am a wretched proofreader; copy editors have saved me from embarrassment over and over again. I read what I intended, what I meant, and very quickly get so caught up in self-love that I lose all track of what I have actually written. A cloud of infatuation hangs over each page. And it all looks so nice, especially with my new printer. I am at my absolute worst when I have to proofread right after I have finished something because I am way too anxious to have it done. My students are the same way; invariably when they hand in their papers, they all could use another close reading. So it occurred to me that I could build in an editing stage, a slow reading task, right as they are to hand in their work. I ask them to perform a small, manageable, specific editing task such as:

- Eliminate ten words that are unnecessary.
- Find one sentence that can be improved and change it.
- Find five word choices that could be improved and write in the better choice.

Usually someone asks, "You mean do it right on the paper?" And I say, "Yes, right on the paper. I don't mind a little mess—you've seen my office." I also say that if they find their writing so perfect that they can't find any changes, to let me have a go at it (usually no takers on this one).

Revising the Technical Descriptions

Much of the writing that conveys technical information is wretchedly written, often actually written with "surgical indifference" to readers. Take for example the "Terms of Service" that came with my new cell phone plan (Virgin Mobile). Here is the first paragraph in twelve densely packed pages:

> The Terms of Service include those general terms ("General Terms") and the terms of your service plan described in the Virgin Mobile Plans, available on our website at www .virginmobileusa.com. These General Terms generally apply

> to the mobile phones and devices we sell and the services we
> offer to our customers, and the Virgin Mobile Service Plans in-
> clude the rates, features and other terms for minutes, messages
> or data you purchase. To the extent that these General Terms
> conflict with any term in the Virgin Mobile Service Plans, these
> General Terms will govern. Please read the Terms of Service
> carefully. (Virgin Mobile, 1)

Say what? Can any of this really be intended for a reader? Do I need to be
told that the "General Terms" will refer to the general terms? And what
does it mean that they are "generally" applied? Are there exceptions?
Couldn't they have written something like this?

> Thank you for selecting a Virgin Mobile Plan. Your **specific
> plan** should indicate the details of that plan—including rates,
> features, and other terms for minutes, messages or data you
> purchase. You can locate the details of your specific plan on our
> website www.virginmobileusa.com.
>
> In this booklet we will describe the **general terms** that gov-
> ern all plans. In the unlikely event that there is a difference be-
> tween these general terms and the terms of your plan, the gen-
> eral terms will prevail. Please read the Terms of Service carefully.

Have I missed anything? My revision uses paragraphs and typographical
features to make key distinctions (specific/general) clearer. And without
being aware of the term, I have used at last two "involvement strategies" in
my revision. According to Peter Elbow, one advantage of speech over formal
writing is the presence of verbal and nonverbal techniques for maintaining
personal contact—something very young writers instinctively do when they
write their reports: "Hello, my name is Sean, and I am going to tell you about
rocks." My opening sentence, thanking the reader, is one involvement strategy, and my creating an agent for the writing, "we," is another. Informational
writing, like this paragraph, becomes very difficult to read when there are
no involvement strategies, no sense of a writer addressing us. Even when we
don't literally revise as I did here, we mentally have to do something like this
when we must decipher lawyer-driven bureaucratic language.

Take the IRS. I send in my tax forms near the beginning of each year, usually around late January, and just about as regularly I get a letter from the IRS a couple of months later, explaining some error I have made. My heart rate goes up when I fish out these very official-looking letters from the mail, and I have to take a few breaths before reading. It usually turns out that I have made some fourth-grade error in arithmetic, but as a writing teacher I am interested in the letters themselves. In Figure 7–2, I have included an especially troublesome one that deserves slow, close reading; in fact, I believe you could teach a good deal about rhetoric from this one letter.

The Internal Revenue Service, essential as it may be, is one of the most detested parts of our government; it is often perceived as rapacious, faceless, arbitrary. In the terms of classical rhetoric, it must work hard to establish "ethos"—to create in readers of letters like this one a sense that the IRS cares about me, that it is taking every effort to be clear and fair, that I am more than a number. Letters like this one are therefore consequential in establishing or impairing a relationship.

And this letter fails miserably.

So I make copies of it, and pose this challenge to students:

> *You are a high-priced writing consultant that is called in by the Internal Revenue Service to examine the effectiveness of their communication with taxpayers. You ask to see some documents and they hand you this letter. As a group, discuss the effectiveness of this letter. Is it clear? Well organized? Does it convey a positive impression of the IRS? If you see problems, what suggestions would you make for improvements?*

Students quickly notice the chaotic arrangement of information and requests. We have to wait until the third paragraph to learn what the problem is; illogically, we have information on how to send the missing information before being informed what is missing. There is even a threat, "We may have to increase the tax you owe" before getting to the very simple problem that occasioned the letter—the failure to send in a schedule that supports an entry (I did the form but forgot to attach it).

Figure 7–2. IRS Form Letter

```
IRS  Department of the Treasury
     Internal Revenue Service
                                    In reply refer to:  0827266036
    ANDOVER  MA  05501-0034         Apr. 26, 2006    LTR 12C   0 S
                                                 200512 30 000
                                                           04867
                                                    BODC: SB



____
      THOMAS R & ELIZABETH G NEWKIRK
____  40 MILL POND RD
      DURHAM  NH  03824




             Social Security Number:
                BATCH 1708,03  08222-056-16614-6

Dear Taxpayer:

We received your Dec. 31, 2005, Form 1040 federal individual
income tax return, but we need more information to process the
return accurately.  Please send us this letter with your reply in
the enclosed envelope within 20 days from the date of this letter.

Please enclose only the information requested and any forms, schedules
or other information required to support your entries.  DO NOT SEND A
COPY OF YOUR RETURN, unless specifically instructed to do so.  We will
issue any refund due to you in about 6 to 8 weeks from the time we
receive your response.  Since we can give you credit for items only if
you give us the information to support them, we may have to increase
the tax you owe or reduce your refund if we do not hear from you.

Please complete Schedule D with information that supports the
entry of $3,773.00 on line 13, Form 1040.

If you have any questions, please call us toll free at 1-800-829-8374
(1-800-829-4059 Telecommunication Device for the Deaf, TDD).  If you
prefer, you may write to us at the address shown at the top of the
first page of this letter.

If you wish to send the information by fax, our fax number is
978-474-5805.  DO NOT SEND AN ADDITIONAL COPY BY MAIL.  Doing so
could delay the processing of your return.  Put your Taxpayer
Identification Number on each page faxed.  Please include a cover
sheet containing the following information:

Date:  _____
Attention:
Name:  Suspense Unit
Control number:  08272
Phone number:  800-829-8374

Your name:  _____
Your Taxpayer Identification Number:  _____
(Social Security Number/Employer Identification Number)
Tax Period:  _____
Number of pages of faxed material:  _____
```

(continues)

Figure 7–2. Continued

```
                                                          0827266036
                                  Apr. 26, 2006    LTR 12C    0 S
                                           200512 30 000
                                                              04868

      THOMAS R & ELIZABETH G NEWKIRK
      40 MILL POND RD
      DURHAM  NH  03824




      The delay that has resulted from this request for additional
      information may have been avoided if you had electronically filed your
      tax return.  For more information about electronic filing, please ask
      your tax preparer or visit our website at www.irs.gov.

      Whenever you write to us, please include your telephone number with
      the area code, the hours we can reach you, and this letter.  Keep
      a copy of this letter for your records.

      Your Telephone Number:  (    )_____   Hours _____

      We apologize for any inconvenience and thank you for your  ,
      cooperation.

                                  Sincerely yours,


                                  Suzanne P. Coppinger
                                  Operations Manager


      Enclosures:
      Copy of this letter
      Envelope
      Schedule D

      BATCH 1708,03
      08222-056-16614-6
```

Students often focus on one sentence that they interpret as scolding: "The delay that has resulted from this request for additional information may have been avoided if you had electronically filed your tax return." This seems extraneous to the purpose of the letter, and the tone is, well, irritating. But I ask students how they might have formulated this request in a more positive way, something like:

> In the future you may want to take advantage of electronic filing—which will enable us to serve you more promptly.

The final sentence in the letter is a last-gasp attempt to put a human face on the letter:

> We apologize for any inconvenience and thank you for your ,
> cooperation.

In the context of the letter, this ending feels jarring and inconsistent with the previous tone of the letter, which is full of directives, where the "inconvenience" was due to my own failure to do an electronic filing. And where did that comma come from?

Other students note other document features: the way the letter looks like a cheap form letter, the two indicators that it is part of "Batch 1708, 03" (how's that for appearing personal?). It is full of long numbers, particularly in the upper right-hand corner, which increase a sense of anonymity. Finally, I am to send the missing document to the "Suspense Unit"—which sounds quite dramatic. Who picks these terms?

One of my students, after our discussion, blurted out: "It just boils down to 'You didn't send us the form for this entry. Can you send it to us?'" But the composition of the letter buries this information, clutters the request with additional information, shifts the tone awkwardly—all of which compromise the "ethos" of the IRS and even the perception of basic competence. I am happy (I guess) to report that subsequent letters on my errors from the IRS are much better.

Making a Good Sentence Better—Examples from Shakespeare to Roosevelt to Kennedy

It is well known that Shakespeare worked from established plots and histories; even at a time of a very different notion of text ownership, he was known as quite a borrower. Instead, he transformed the language and characterization of this earlier work, a process that we can almost see at work in his play *Antony and Cleopatra*, which is heavily based on the Greek biographer Plutarch's *Lives of Noble Greeks and Romans*. Plutarch himself knew a good scene when he came across it, and few were more dramatic than Cleopatra's trip down the Nile river to meet Antony after he had established himself as the Roman ruler of Egypt. It was so good that Shakespeare lifted entire sections of the description, but he clearly improved the last sentence in Plutarch's description, which described how people abandoned Antony to see the arrival of Cleopatra, leaving the mighty Roman leader alone in the marketplace. Here is what Shakespeare read from Plutarch:

> Some of them followed the barge all alongst the river's side; others ran outside the city to see her coming in. So that in th' end there ran such multitudes of people one after another to see her, that Antony was left post alone in the market place, in his imperial seat to give audience; and there was a rumor that the goddess Venus was come to play with the God Bacchus for the general good of all Asia. (1690)

It is a great moment, vividly captured, but here is what Shakespeare does with it:

>   . . . The city cast
> Her people out upon her. And Antony,
> Enthoned i' the market place did sit alone,
> Whistling to the air, which, but for vacancy,
> Had gone to gaze on Cleopatra too,
> And made a gap in nature. (1,234)

One can almost imagine a thought process here, Shakespeare seeking out action or a figure of speech to emphasize Antony's abandonment. So he has him whistle, and more, he is whistling to the air, which itself would prefer to leave the marketplace but to do so would leave a vacuum or "gap in nature." *Even the air wants to leave.* Comparisons of single sentences like these can illustrate the great Elizabethan love of conceits and figures of speech that still push us to stretch our imaginative capacities.

We can use the same contrastive approach to look at two of the most famous sentences in U.S. history. One is the opening to Franklin Delano Roosevelt's December 8, 1941, speech declaring war on Japan after the bombing of Pearl Harbor. The typescript (Figure 7–3) of the marked-up speech draft, available online, reveals several changes in the original text,

Figure 7–3. FDR's December 8, 1941, Marked-Up Typescript Speech

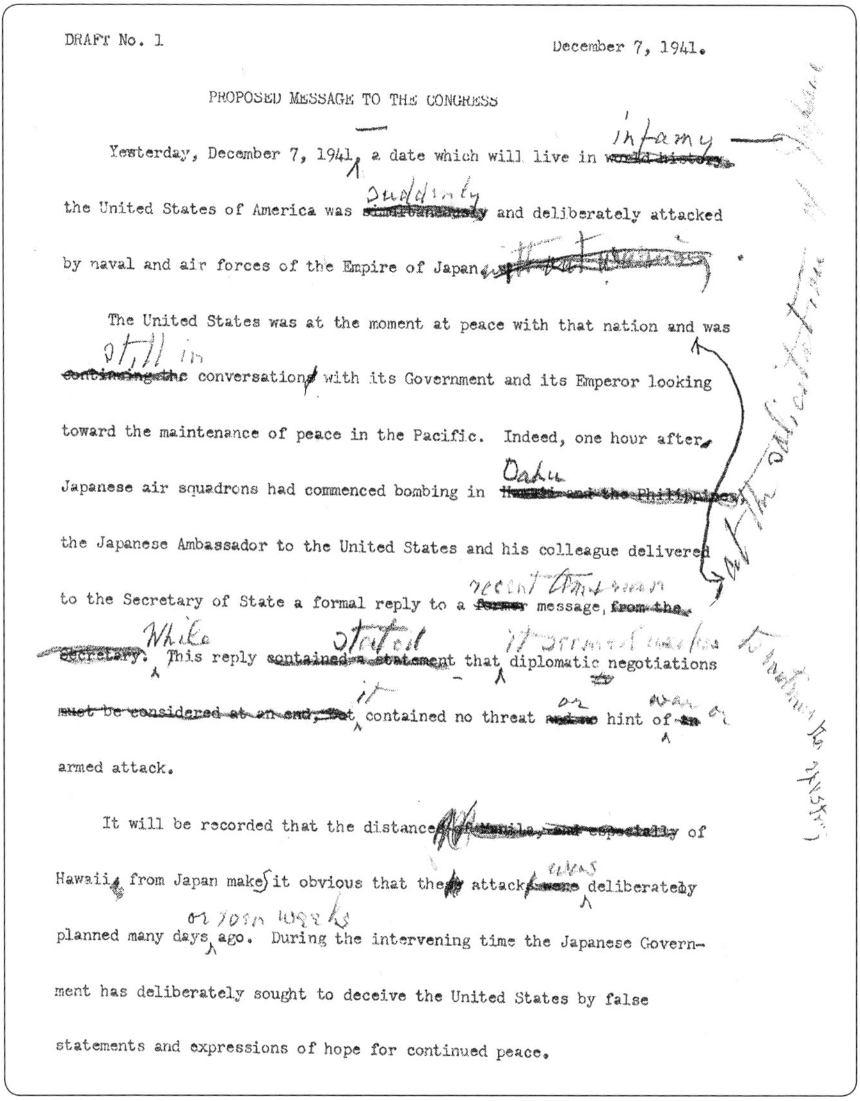

DRAFT No. 1 December 7, 1941.

PROPOSED MESSAGE TO THE CONGRESS

Yesterday, December 7, 1941, a date which will live in ~~world history~~ infamy the United States of America was ~~simultaneously~~ suddenly and deliberately attacked by naval and air forces of the Empire of Japan.

The United States was at the moment at peace with that nation and was ~~continuing the~~ still in conversations with its Government and its Emperor looking toward the maintenance of peace in the Pacific. Indeed, one hour after Japanese air squadrons had commenced bombing in ~~Hawaii and the Philippines~~ Oahu the Japanese Ambassador to the United States and his colleague delivered to the Secretary of State a formal reply to a ~~former~~ recent American message, ~~from the Secretary~~. While this reply ~~contained a statement~~ stated that diplomatic negotiations ~~must be considered at an end, but~~ it contained no threat ~~and no~~ or hint of ~~an~~ war or armed attack.

It will be recorded that the distance ~~of Manila, and especially~~ of Hawaii, from Japan makes it obvious that the attack ~~were~~ was deliberately planned many days or even weeks ago. During the intervening time the Japanese Government has deliberately sought to deceive the United States by false statements and expressions of hope for continued peace.

each of which changed the effect of the speech. Here is what he originally dictated to his secretary:

> Yesterday, December 7, 1941, a date that will live in world history, the United States of America was simultaneously and deliberately attacked by naval and air forces of the Empire of Japan.

He added *without warning* to the end of this sentence, but crossed it out. The other changes, three of them, resulted in this historic opening:

> Yesterday, December 7, 1941—a date that will live in infamy—
> the United States was suddenly and deliberately attacked by
> naval and air forces of the Empire of Japan.

The revised letter is more forceful: the dashes give emphasis to the central claim of the speech, the culpability of Japan. And his substitution of *infamy* for *world history* turns a neutral claim into a morally charged one, and one that is memorably resonant in the oral speech. His substitution of *suddenly* for *simultaneously* avoids a confusion about what is happening simultaneously (attacks on planes, airfields) that he probably didn't want to get into. But *suddenly and deliberately* reinforces the brutally dramatic and intentional acts of the Japanese. Each of the changes, small as they seem on the typescript, brings the speech to a moral pitch needed to mobilize a country to war.

The most famous line from John F. Kennedy's presidency, and one of the most famous in American history, came near the end of his inaugural address: "Ask not what your country can do for you; ask what you can do for your country." It was one that inspired many of his younger listeners to public service. But the recently released early written draft showed that Kennedy did not word it this way at the beginning. He wrote:

> Ask not what your country is going to do for you; ask what you
> can do for your country.

The same idea, but clearly inferior to the line that became famous. The line as delivered is more compact—and parallel. We don't know, at least I don't, the process Kennedy went through to revise this sentence, but it is probable that he didn't use any "rule" about parallel construction—more likely he *heard* the problem; and by the same token his audience didn't need a grammar lesson to appreciate (and venerate) the revised sentence. I suspect that we all innately possess an awareness of sentence rhythm and an instinctive responsiveness to the revised parallel version, with the two parts of the sentence repeating in inverse order (which is one reason for reading our writing aloud—to make use of our ear for language). The repetition of *can* makes all the difference. It is doubtful the line would have made its way into history and legend in the original version.

But the best examples of revising sentences can come from students sharing their own changes and explaining the improvements.

Rubbing Out the Words

In his book *The Child's Concept of Story*, Arthur Applebee reports on an exchange between the researcher and a six-year-old student, Stephen. Stephen is asked to pick a story he doesn't like and he nominates "Sleeping Beauty." The interview continues:

> RESEARCHER: If you were telling "Sleeping Beauty," could you change it so that you would like it?
>
> STEPHEN: No.
>
> RESEARCHER: Why not? Is it alright to make changes in stories?
>
> STEPHEN: No.
>
> RESEARCHER: Do you think you could make it better?
>
> STEPHEN: No.
>
> RESEARCHER: Why not?
>
> STEPHEN: Because you can't rub out the words. (39)

Stephen seems to be saying that texts are fixed and authoritative, beyond tinkering and revising. He can't see through the seeming *inevitability* of texts—the deceptive ways in which words evenly follow words on the page, seemingly without pause, page after page of them. One second grader, Alan, in Donald Graves' research project in the late 1970s, put it this way: "Before I ever wrote a book I used to think that there was a big machine, and they typed the title and then the machine went until the book was done." Many of my own college students will refer to a "they" who wrote a book, even when the single author is named on the cover, as if it was the product of some impersonal conglomerate—and to be fair some of their textbooks *are* created that way. They are *developed* and not written. But writing changed that view for Alan:

> Now I look at a book and know that a guy wrote it. And it's been his project for a long time. After the guy writes it, he probably thinks about questions people will ask him and revises it the way I do and xeroxes it to read to about six editors. Then he fixes it up the way they say. (Newkirk, *Young Writers*, 457)

The act of writing, and in Alan's case publishing to an audience of peers, demystifies writing itself; it pulls back the veil on the process, reveals authorship to be a matter of making choices, altering choices. Insiders like Alan know this. Writing is a demystified human act, a set of decisions and revisions. Thus, while reading can make us better writers—writing can make us better, more discerning, more human readers.

And sadly, writing is always an approximation of what we hoped to do. As Michael Cunningham writes:

> A novel, any novel, if it's any good, is not only a slightly disappointing translation of the novelist's grandest intentions, it is also the most finished draft he could come up with before he collapsed from exhaustion. It's all I can do not to go from bookstore to bookstore with a pen, grabbing my books from the shelves, crossing out certain lines I've come to regret and inserting better ones.

My own colleague, the noted poet Charles Simic, is known to fiddle with his poems directly on the page of *The New Yorker* where they appeared.

Something similar occurred in Ellen Karelitz's first-grade class a number of years ago. Several students were reading a basal version of the folktale "The Belling of the Cat," in which, at least in the original version, mice put a bell on a cat to provide warning. But in the basal version, for some reason (perhaps to simplify vocabulary), none of the mice are brave enough to act. Simon read the ending which went like this:

> "Can you get the bell on the cat?"
> "I cannot get the bell on the cat."
> "Can you?"

"Not I."
"Not I."
"It cannot work."
"We cannot get the bell on the cat."

Simon's response to this defeatist ending was "Who wrote this?" Ellen explained that no one person really wrote it, but it was probably done by a group of authors. To which he responded, "You mean adults wrote this?"

Ellen encouraged him to think of a different ending and, after discussions with classmates, he wrote:

All the mice were sad. One of the mice said, "Wait!" And he told them. They got into the medicine cabinet. They got the sleeping powder and they put it in the cat's food and when the cat came he ate some, he fell asleep and they put the bell on the cat and now when the cat comes, it rings. (Karelitz, 106)

Ellen bound Simon's new—and clearly superior—ending into the book, and she added his name to the title page.

You can, after all, rub out the words—and choose better ones.

Chapter 8

OPENING A TEXT
ELABORATING

The trouble with poetry is
that it encourages the writing of more poetry
—BILLY COLLINS, "THE TROUBLE WITH POETRY"

And what was worst of all, she had no opinions of any sort. She saw objects
about her and understood what she saw, but could not form an opinion about
them, and did not know what to talk about. How awful it was not to have any
opinions! One sees a bottle, for instance, or the rain, or a peasant driving in
his cart, but what the bottle is for, or the rain, or the peasant, and what is the
meaning of it, one can't say, and could not even for a thousand roubles.
—ANTON CHEKHOV, "THE DARLING"

This chapter will continue on the theme of reading like a writer. In the previous chapter, we focused on learning craft through careful, attentive reading. In this one, we will focus on ways of reading—both our own writing and the writing of others—that generate writing. It is premised on the belief that we rarely simply *comprehend*, a word with root meanings of "grasp" or "hold." We act on it in some way—we explain it, teach it, quote it, perform it, evaluate it, analyze it, allow it to call up associated experiences and ideas. We create alongside the writer. Unlike Chekhov's pathetic character, we have opinions about it.

One of the most basic problems of inexperienced writers is generating text; they experience constant anxiety about meeting page limits, about finding enough to write, of creating what Erasmus called "copia." There is an ironclad correlation between length and writing quality on many writing assessments. Some find this a scandal, but it may really only reflect the truism that better writers have a way of finding material to write about.

> *...fluency in writing, as in speech, comes from being responsive to what is happening.*

The question of how writers find and develop material is, of course, a huge one, beyond the scope of any chapter, even any book. This chapter will look at only one aspect—the generative ways in which writers read. An embarrassing example from my own dating past may help explain what I'll be getting at. I suspect I wasn't alone in being terrified that there would be nothing to talk about on dates, that we would sit in uncomfortable fidgeting silence for long periods of time. So, I would rehearse topics (the Cleveland Indians, work at Brookside Park, high school teachers) to talk about as I drove to pick up the unfortunate young woman. This strategy, to put it mildly, did not work. It felt unnatural and stilted even to me—not to mention that I quickly ran through all my topics. I would have been much better off if I had relaxed, listened, asked questions, and been spontaneous; if I had trusted conversation, and myself (and her), more.

Similarly, writers can plan in advance—create lists, outlines, webs, whatever—but fluency in writing, as in speech, comes from being responsive to what is happening. It involves a special conversational way of reading, of allowing writing to invite more writing—a process Don Murray called "listening to the text." In much of his writing about process, the emerging text is not an inanimate set of symbols on the page—it is active. It "instructs" the writer. This was not reading to comprehend, but reading to create.

> The writer has to develop new forms of reading, to read loosely at first, to give the piece of writing space so that embryonic patterns of meaning which are making shadowy appearance can

have time to become clear. Writers have to learn to listen for the almost imperceptible sounds which may develop into a voice they do not expect. As the meanings come clear, the voices grow stronger. The writer has to read with increasing care, has to be critical, even surgical, but not at first. ("Writing as Process," 14)

One of his great, unfulfilled hopes was that there would be collaborations of reading and writing researchers to study this special and generative way of attending to our own writing.

This chapter then will explore two questions:

1. How can students read their own writing in a way that helps us create fuller, more elaborated texts?

2. How can we use the writing of others to help us elaborate writing? What strategies are there for unpacking and opening up quotations?

"... And Am Not Yet Born"

One of the great British novels, *The Life and Opinions of Tristram Shandy, Gentleman* (Sterne), is full of laments about the difficulty of composing a straightforward narrative; it's a novel about the impossibility of writing a novel. In Chapter 14, the narrator acknowledges that despite six weeks of hard work, he hasn't gotten to the point of his own birth. He explains his problem this way:

> For, if he is a man of the least spirit, he will have fifty deviations from a straight line to make with this or that party as he goes along, which he can no way avoid. He will have views and prospects to himself perpetually soliciting his eye, which he can no more help standing still to look at than he can fly; he will moreover have various
>
> Accounts to reconcile:
> Anecdotes to pick up:
> Inscriptions to make out:
> Stories to weave in:

> Traditions to sift:
> Personages to call upon:
> Panegyrics to paste up on the door (28)

"In short," he concludes, "there is no end of it." To write in a direct, linear fashion is to be oblivious to the distractive possibilities and pleasures of living; it is to go about in blinders. It is to be without "spirit."

Reading can also embody this digressive spirit and merge into writing. The text can activate digression, meditation, reflection. Take the example of comedian Mike Birbiglia reading a sweetener packet:

> Other people read books continuously, in a block of time. Whereas the way I read is a conversation with the author, who's not leaving me space to talk back. Like, what are the ingredients for Splenda? [starts reading sweetener packet] Dextrose . . . malto-dextrin . . . I don't even get to the end before I'm like, "What's the difference between dextrose and maltodextrin? Are they brewed in the same laboratory? Do I like sugar? I like sugar. But I'm not a sweets person. I'm more of, like, a carbs person. I like hearty foods, I like macaroni and cheese." Meanwhile the packet's not engaging in the conversation! That's why I can't read. (Katz)

But of course he *is* reading.

This emphasis on digression, on listening to the text, on writing with "spirit," is surely open to the objection that it violates the reader's need for focus and order. We read to get, to "comprehend," the writer's message—we write to convey a thought, not to create a Rorschach image. And if you look at some models for writing school essays, they appear to be cages within cages; the unruliness of writing is contained by the thesis, the topic sentences, and, lest there be too much divergence, by a concluding paragraph that drives home the point of the essay. It looks like the traditional, 1950s-style corporate structure—the CEO at top, various divisional managers reporting to him, and lower-level workers reporting to them. So, what is wrong with this picture? In fact, isn't this the kind of writing that colleges and SAT readers want? Don't writers need to know the form before they deviate from it?

These tight structures radically underestimate the moves a reader can make—and wants to make. Someone who watches *The Wire* or *The Sopranos* in her spare time is not likely to be thrown, really thrown, by a paragraph or two that are not tightly connected to a thesis; in fact, she may welcome that kind of exploration. It is possible to be too focused. After all, the great lesson of art in the twentieth century is the expanding capacity of the viewer/reader/listener for dissonance. One might also argue, more conservatively, that even if the end goal is to write a tight argument, the writer still needs to work from excess, to generate more than can be used. The very act of organizing implies an element of chaos to be organized; no mess, no need to create order.

The argument that students need to learn the "form" of the essay before they can alter it begs the question of just what the essay form is—and who's doing the violating. Here is Clifford Geertz on the essay:

> For making detours and going by sideroads, nothing is more convenient than the essay form. One can take off in almost any direction, certain that if the thing does not work out one can turn back and start over in some other at moderate cost. . . . Wandering into smaller sideroads and wider detours does little harm, for progress is not expected to be relentlessly forward, but winding and improvisational, coming out where it comes out. And when there is nothing more to say on a subject at the moment, or perhaps altogether, the matter can be simply dropped. "Works are not finished," as Valery said, "they are abandoned." (*Local Knowledge*, 6)

In other words, digression and exploration are inherent to the "form," certainly as developed by Montaigne. What we present as the school essay, particularly the almost anal concern for control, misrepresents the form (and the reader).

We can also make a developmental case in favor of digression and generativity—that as Alfred North Whitehead claimed an "age of romance" needs to precede an "age of precision." Young athletes, for example, often don't have their skills fully under control—they will try passes and shots they are not able to accomplish; they will improvise in sometimes disastrous ways. Good coaches don't train this excess completely out of them. Good young writers are often excessive writers, purple writers, who pile on the adjectives, who push descriptions to the limit of what they can imagine and what a reader can take in. They want to write epics. The wise Roman teacher Quintilian may have put it best:

> Let that age be daring, invent much, and delight in what it invents, though it be often not sufficiently severe and correct. The remedy for exuberance is easy; barrenness is incurable by any labor. That temper in boys will afford me little hope in which mental effort is prematurely restrained by judgment. I like what is produced to be extremely copious, profuse beyond the limits of propriety. (303)

In other words, the argument that students need tight forms from which they can later deviate seems to me backward; they need to experience the human capacity for generation and excess; they need to be in touch with their own associative resources. I would extend Quintilian to say that *at any age* we need this attitude early in the writing process. As many before me have noted, the great enemy of productivity is a premature concern for audience that inhibits this production.

Still, improvisation, even digression, is a skill. I have always been mystified by jazz musicians who can take a motif or "line" from a popular song and build an eight- or ten-minute performance that was not planned in advance and can never be repeated. I asked one of my friends with a background in music about the magical skill, and his response is that it wasn't magic. He said, "It's like, for example, you talking about writing. You have a language for it, a background. You talk for hours about it without any preparation. It's a field of references you know. The process is similar for jazz musicians."

Part of this improvisational skill—which is what I take Murray to mean by "listening to the text"—is a capacity for self-prompting, building off what has been written. For experienced writers, these moves can be so automatic that it *feels* as though the text is "informing" the writer. At other times, the prompting is more deliberate. Without the capacity to self-prompt, writers can only rely on the initial plan and, like me on my dates, they quickly run out of material. This generative, creative way of reading the evolving text accounts for the pleasure of writing—the sense of discovery, even learning, that comes in the process. It also can account for the pleasure of reading, the feeling of spontaneity, of being present with a mind and sensibility that is in motion, that is not still and preformulated.

To name the various prompts we create for ourselves can make the process seem too calculated, when for experienced writers there is a syntax of elaboration that seems, often, as automatic as the ability to construct sentences. But we can name some of these moves. As we write we may ask ourselves:

What happens next?

What does it look like, feel like, smell like?

How can I restate that?

What's my reaction to that?

What example or experience can I call up to illustrate that?

What parts of my prior reading can I bring to bear on that?

What comparison can I make that makes that clearer?

Why does that matter?

What do I mean by that?

Who else would agree with that? Disagree? What "counterdiscourse" can I bring in?

How can I qualify the statement? What are the exceptions?

How does that fit into larger debates or controversies?

Obviously these questions imply knowledge of the topic—you can't "write writing." To make connections in your writing, you need something to connect to; it is well and good to argue for Montaigne's "essay" but Montaigne had such a "funded" mind that he could do all that traveling. So, just as a fund of prior knowledge is crucial for reading comprehension, it is even more vital for writing.

Prompts like the ones above, which are only a sampling, allow us to access what we know and build connections we could not have anticipated. To the extent that these prompts are internalized and made habitual, a writer can become fluent. Collectively, they comprise the most important cultural capital that we can pass on to our children and students. Studies of parenting show that almost from infancy, some parents begin to build this connective tissue of thinking: "And what happened next?" "How did that make you feel?" "What was your favorite part?" "Why did you like it?" And later on to prompts like "What makes you say that?" "How would you respond to those who say . . . ?" "What do you mean by . . . ?" In his study of "choice words" that promote learning, Peter Johnston identifies several prompts that extend thinking, that model a kind of consecutiveness so critical to writing. Among them are:

ALTERNATIVE THINKING—"What else?" "Are there any other ways to think about that?" "Any other opinions?"

EMPATHIZING—"How do you think she feels about that?"

CAUSATION—"Why?"

HYPOTHESIZING AND SPECULATING—"I wonder . . ." "What if . . . ?"

COMPARING—"That's like . . ."

One of the most powerful strategies he offers is silence, mental space for learners to extend their thinking, what I have called earlier the "blank probe"—as if to say, "Tell me more, I know you have something to say. I can wait." (Great teachers, in my experience, don't seem rushed.) To the student immersed as a child in these kinds of interactions, the elaborative moves of academic writing can feel second nature. With inexperienced writers, and those for whom this probing may be less instinctive, it is crucial that they see it demonstrated, in classroom discussion and in responses to their writing.

"As Long as There Is Ink and Paper in the World"

No one has demonstrated this generative process of reading more effectively than Montaigne himself, particularly in the revisions he made near the end of his life. By then, he had already published two highly successful versions of his essays, the second a huge volume with margins of about three inches. In his last years, he compulsively reread this volume, making additions in the margins, sometimes pasting notes onto the pages, the forerunner of the sticky note—in effect, he wrote the equivalent of an entire book in those margins, inserting personal details, new quotes, sometimes qualifying or even contradicting what he had said before. (Figure 8–1 is a facsimile of one of his pages with a long insertion in the margins.) He very rarely deleted anything he had written earlier, claiming that he was skeptical that he had grown wiser and that his earlier thoughts were part of the self he is creating in the essays. In his view, there was really no end to the essays; he claimed that they could go on "as long as there was ink and paper in the world." Only his own death in 1592 ended his expansions.

We can sense this process of revision in two of the 168 additions he made to his last and most memorable essay, "On Experience." He is remarking, in the published version, on the way his severe bouts of kidney stones brings him close to death and makes "her" familiar in a way—all of which prompts an extension of his thinking as he continues the figure of speech. I italicized his marginal addition:

> Although you may not throw your arms around Death's neck, you do, once a month, shake her by the hand. *That gives you more reason to hope that Death will snatch you one day without warning and that, having so often brought you as far as the jetty, one morning, unexpectedly, when you are trusting you are still on the same terms, you and your trust will have crossed the Styx.* (1,240)

As readers, we can sense the way in which this image of death as a companion, one that you shake hands with on a monthly basis, could extend in his mind to a final meeting that he is, by now, well prepared for.

Often Montaigne used his additions to add greater emphasis and imagery to the points he is making, and never as memorably as in the next to last edition of "On Experience" in which he comments on the difficult

Figure 8–1. Montaigne Manuscript

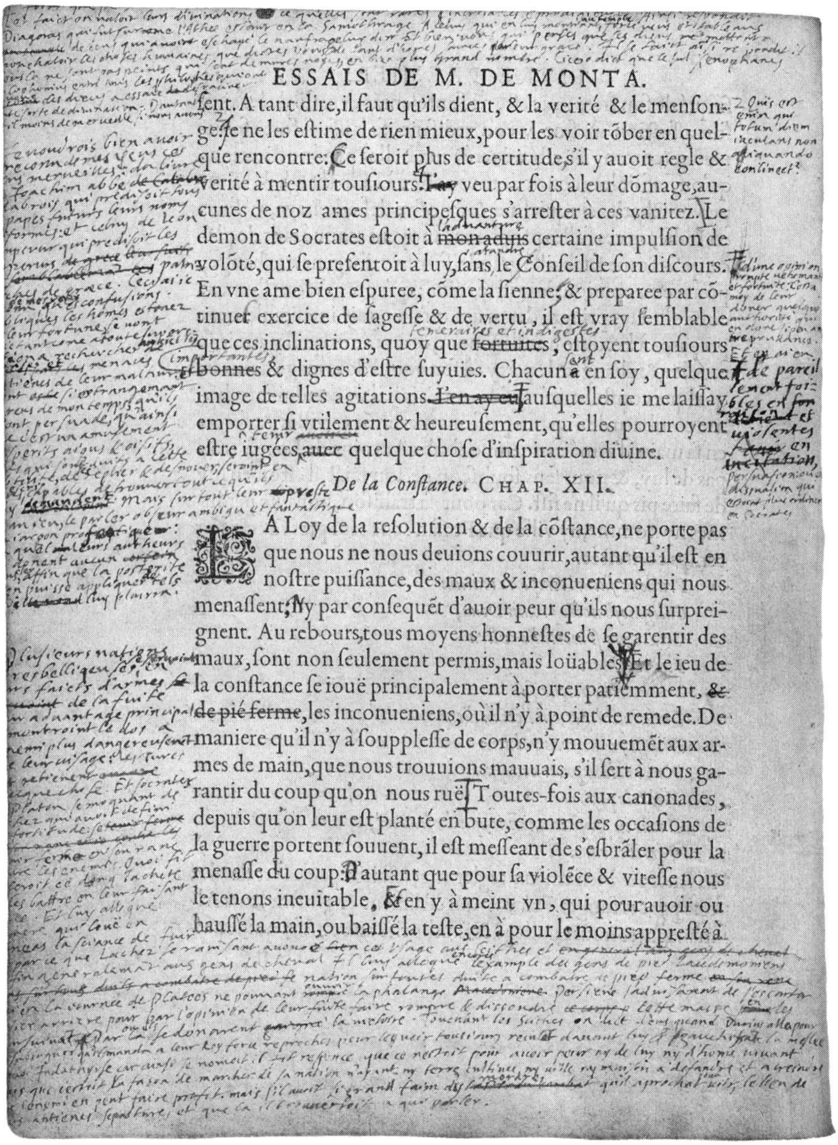
ESSAIS DE M. DE MONTA.

sent. A tant dire, il faut qu'ils dient, & la verité & le mensonge. Ie ne les estime de rien mieux, pour les voir tõber en quelque rencontre. Ce seroit plus de certitude, s'il y auoit regle & verité à mentir tousiours. I'ay veu par fois à leur dõmage, aucunes de noz ames principesques s'arrester à ces vanitez. Le demon de Socrates estoit à mon aduis certaine impulsion de volõté, qui se presentoit à luy, sans le Conseil de son discours. En vne ame bien espuree, cõme la sienne, & preparee par cõtinuel exercice de sagesse & de vertu, il est vray semblable que ces inclinations, quoy que fortuites, estoyent tousiours bonnes & dignes d'estre suyuies. Chacun a en soy, quelque image de telles agitations. I'en ay eu ausquelles ie me laissay emporter si vtilement & heureusement, qu'elles pourroyent estre iugees, auec quelque chose d'inspiration diuine.

De la Constance. CHAP. XII.

LA Loy de la resolution & de la cõstance, ne porte pas que nous ne nous deuions couurir, autant qu'il est en nostre puissance, des maux & inconueniens qui nous menassent, ny par consequẽt d'auoir peur qu'ils nous surpreignent. Au rebours, tous moyens honnestes de se garentir des maux, sont non seulement permis, mais loüables. Et le ieu de la constance se iouë principalement à porter patiemment, & de pié ferme, les inconueniens, où il n'y à point de remede. De maniere qu'il n'y à soupplesse de corps, n'y mouuemẽt aux armes de main, que nous trouuions mauuais, s'il sert à nous garantir du coup qu'on nous ruë. Toutes-fois aux canonades, depuis qu'on leur est planté en bute, comme les occasions de la guerre portent souuent, il est messeant de s'esbräler pour la menasse du coup: d'autant que pour sa violẽce & vitesse nous le tenons ineuitable, & en y à meint vn, qui pour auoir ou haussé la main, ou baissé la teste, en à pour le moins apresté à business of self-acceptance and our impulse to imagine ourselves grander than we are:

> We seek other attributes because we do not understand the use of our own; and, having no knowledge of what is within, we sally forth outside ourselves. *A fine thing to get up on stilts: for even on stilts we must ever walk on our legs! And upon the highest throne in the world, we are seated, still, upon our arses.* (1,269)

In this addition, Montaigne illustrates an abstract point made in the previous edition, with a graphic comparison that grounds his point in an unforgettable image. No wonder Shakespeare stole from him.

Montaigne, with his wide inviting margins, offers a strategy for teaching revision that our inservice program has used with writers at all levels. In effect, we reproduce those margins; we ask students to tape their papers onto a much bigger sheet of paper. Then we discuss ways in which they can add comments and details in that margin. These additions could include:

- details (e.g., fuller descriptions of participants, setting) that have been left out
- dialogue
- internal reactions and thoughts of individuals (including the writer)
- a "naysayer" who questions your point or position
- whole new episodes or anecdotes that can help develop the point of the writing
- connections to other things you have read or experienced
- new evidence

The writer is not obligated to include all of this side addition, but, just as for Montaigne, the technique, and all that open space, invites elaboration.

"But the Handles Are Loose"

Quotation is often treated as a technical task with rules for indentation, punctuation, and the like. Or it is treated as a way to "back up" an argument, to give solidity to points the writer is making. It is, of course, all these things. But for many writers, it is something more personal and generative than that. It is an act of deep affection and respect. We typically "quote up" and include the exact words of other writers who make their points better, more eloquently, more authoritatively than we do. There are some quotes that we remain profoundly loyal to, that we return to again and again, that continue to open up new territory for us. The quotation is something more than evidence, a way to "back up" a point; it is generative as well. It helps the writer move forward. It invites us to talk back—to extend, paraphrase, qualify, agree, disagree, interpret, to find examples from our reading and experience.

Montaigne, one of the greatest (and most self-conscious) quoters in all of literature, makes this comment about those who have only an external relationship to the material they quote:

> They will handle that material like a man who fears getting
> scalded; they dare not show it in different light, or context,
> nor deepen it. Give it the tiniest shaking and it slips away from
> them; then, strong and beautiful though it be, they surrender
> it to you. They have beautiful weapons, but the handles are
> loose! (1,062)

One way in which inexperienced writers "surrender" quotations to us is with the hanging quote; they have made a point, backed it up with the quote—and they just leave us there as readers. These don't own the quote, don't exhibit any thinking about it—it doesn't generate anything. They have found a way into it, but not a way out of it.

The use of quotations to generate writing has long been a mainstay of instruction, revived recently in the SAT writing prompts. Several years ago, I found in the Harvard University Archives a list of topics that Edward Channing gave his students from 1823 to his retirement in 1851 (among these were the ones that Thoreau wrote to). Often there would be some quote from Milton or Lucretius or Southey that students were expected to write about. Unlike Chekhov's "Darling," they were expected to have opinions on everything—the responsibility of kings, the gold rush, the writing style of Seneca and Cicero, Hamilton versus Jefferson, whether old age made you wiser. Here is an example from about the time Thoreau was a student:

> "There is in the higher class a sickly craving after everything foreign and an unusual affectation of scorn for everything native."
> Ancients just the opposite. (Channing)

Actually, it would have been a good topic for Thoreau. Later in the century, one of Channing's successors, Barrett Wendell, invited his students to pick a line of poetry from Palgrave's *Golden Treasury* and use it as a "point of departure" for narrative and descriptive writing. (The technique of working from a given line is a standard exercise in poetry workshops.) Fundamental to this approach is the potential of quotations to stir memory and provoke writing. This instruction mirrors the religious practice of working from a short verse in developing a sermon. This practice is sometimes called "opening a text," an expression that appears in the New Testament, near the end of the Gospel of Luke.

"They will handle that material like a man who fears getting scalded...."

—Montaigne

So how does a writer read to be provoked? A good place to start is with one of the great documents in the Civil Rights Movement and a classic piece of persuasion—Martin Luther King Jr.'s "Letter from a Birmingham Jail." This letter, actually an extended essay, was written while King was in jail for demonstrating in Birmingham, Alabama, and he began it along the margins of the *New York Times*, later finishing on scraps of paper and finally a legal pad given to him by his lawyer. In the letter, he responds to a statement by several Alabama clergy criticizing those who led the Birmingham demonstrators. One can almost construct a process of provocation in King's letter: he focuses on judgmental terms used by the clergy to describe the demonstrations—"extreme," "untimely," "outsiders." He interrogates and contests these terms, contesting the meaning that the ministers had given to them. For example, he has this to say about the "timeliness" of his work:

> Frankly, I have never yet engaged in a direct-action campaign that was "well-timed" according to the timetable of those who have not suffered unduly from the disease of segregation. For years now I have heard the word, "Wait!" It rings in the ear of every Negro with piercing familiarity. This "Wait" has almost always meant "Never." (656)

He returns to this theme later in the letter and makes this profound and eloquent argument:

> All that is said here grows out of a tragic misconception of time. It is the strangely rational notion that there is something in the very flow of time that will inevitably cure all ills. Actually, time is neutral. It can be used either destructively or constructively. . . . We must come to see that human progress never rolls in on wheels of inevitability. It comes through the tireless efforts of men willing to be the co-workers with God, and without this hard work time itself becomes an ally of the forces of social stagnation. (660)

With the term *extremist,* he inverts the meaning of the term so he can embrace it:

> I must admit that I was initially disappointed to be so categorized.
> But as I continued to think about the matter I gradually gained a bit of satisfaction from being considered an extremist. Was not Jesus an extremist in love: "Love your enemies, and bless those who curse you, do good to them that hate you, and pray for them that despitefully use you." Was not Amos an extremist for justice: "Let justice roll down like waters and righteousness like an everflowing stream." (661)

He continues with other "extremists"—Martin Luther, John Bunyan, Abraham Lincoln, Thomas Jefferson—thus claiming that what he calls "creative extremism" is part of his political and religious heritage. King, of course, is trained in a tradition of close, scriptural reading, and in the case of this letter, one can follow his own meditation on the key terms in the minister's letter. One lesson we can learn from his process is that a key action in "opening a text" is to *interrogate the key words*. Lacking the ability (or will) to do this interrogation, readers are lulled into acceptance—and silence.

As Erasmus wrote in his book *On Copia*, another key to expansion is mastery of the example, the readiness to call up pertinent stories, experiences, fables, parables. The assumption is that the writer has a "well-stocked" mind. And the same could be said of these SAT prompts. To accomplish this writing, a writer needs to be in the habit of reflection—of treating experiences and reading as exemplary, meaningful, memorable, as speaking to wider issues of concern. In his hugely influential *Aids to Reflection*, Samuel Taylor Coleridge begins by noting that truths easily become clichés, so "true" that they lose their power and lie "bedridden in the dormitory of the soul." He recommends reflection as the means of animating these truths:

> There is one sure way of giving freshness and importance to the most commonplace maxims—that of reflecting on them in direct reference to our own state of conduct, to our own past and future being. (1)

He claims that the best plan is to "dwell at home." It is surely the case that we cannot expect the common core of cultural knowledge and reference that was common in the nineteenth century and earlier, but if students have developed the habit of reflection, the analytic essay becomes manageable, even meaningful. An example is *framed* or pulled from the flow of activity, given form and significance; it becomes instructive, illustrative, and ready for use. According to James Britton, we become our own "spectators." A minister I know claims that in preparing for her Sunday preaching, she has a "sermonic eye" for details, stories, experiences, memories that can help her explicate the passage for the week. "You prepare with a Bible in one hand and the newspaper in the other."

There are few more important writing skills—none in my view—than the capacity to ground an observation in a story that gives that idea a sense of presence, of human reality. We humans are just not good at dealing with abstractions for too long (which makes the reading of John Dewey such a challenge). My colleague Charles Simic writes:

> The present is the only place where we can experience the eternal. The eternal shrinks to the size of the present because only the present can be humanly grasped. (56)

He argues that the goal of the poet, particularly the lyric poet, is to offer as closely as possible "the experience of the naked moment" (55). I would add that expository writers must also be able to create the sense of presence, of being there, if their ideas are to be convincing and even understood (even remembered). Exposition that is unleavened by description and narration is almost intolerable to read.

Take this example from an essay by a first-year college student, a profile of her severely autistic brother who is only able to cope with his world by focusing on basketball, particularly dribbling. In one memorable paragraph we see (and feel) how fragile this world is:

> There are times when Christopher does not have the chance to put up this protective wall. I came home one evening with a group of friends, all of whom were strangers to Chris. He was sitting on the rocking chair in our living room, watching a video of NBA Super Slams, part of his bedtime routine. My friends and I entered the room, and said "hello" to him. Suddenly every muscle in his little body became a rock. He was straining to keep focusing on the television, on the ball in the hands of the player in the video, but he could not ignore the faces, voices, and bodies that were surrounding him in the room. The walls were closing in. I could see the tears welling up in his eyes and the amount of force he was exerting while trying to hold them back. And then he let go. He gave up and the tears began to flow like the water from a dam that had just been broken. He fled from the room, screaming, and collapsed into our mother's arms. (Daly, 25)

This paragraph makes *present* the panic of her brother, the way that a simple "hello" can disrupt the routines he relies on. I would argue that the capacity to recall experience in such indelible moments, these "spots of time" as Wordsworth called them, is just as essential for our psychological health as it is for writing. These memories, these souvenirs, place us in our own pasts; they give us a past. And it is simply perverse, in my view, to teach writing in a way that separates description and narration (treating them as elementary modes) from analytic writing.

The Art of Attention: Lessons from Scriptural Reading

When Georgia O'Keeffe began painting her huge and evocative flowers, she explained her decision this way:

> Nobody sees a flower, really—so I said to myself I'll paint what I see—but I'll paint it big. And they will be surprised into taking their time to look at it.

We don't see flowers because we "know" what they look like. We "see" this preformed mental image, a process that Walker Percy has called "the loss of the creature." We visit the Grand Canyon, look at its vastness, and come away satisfied. "Yes, it looks just like the picture." Reading specialists claim with obvious justification that readers need to activate schema, but the dilemma arises that if we simply project our schema (those images of the Grand Canyon) onto what we see—we are only seeing what we expect. We operate in a closed circle. When Cézanne boasted that he would "astonish Paris with an apple," he was claiming to disrupt this automatic process of identification. But as O'Keeffe notes, this process of estrangement requires the viewer to take time, to be open to surprise. It requires an attitude of receptivity and not merely the projection of expectation. Similarly, there are reading traditions, particularly religious practices of reading sacred texts, that cultivate a sustained attitude of openness.

As I have noted earlier, the term *comprehension* seems ill suited to describe this type of reading. Although we are not bound by etymology, the roots of *comprehension* have to do with containment, grasping or holding, or "thought-getting." The word is in the same family as *compression* or *compress*, which encloses or presses in upon. We *extract* meaning and information from the text—it is there, we reach in, get it, and hold it. Virtually all the testing we do is based on this model. But the most powerful, the most personally meaningful reading that we do is nothing at all like this; it entails a different mind-set entirely, a vulnerability, humility, and openness, what Wordsworth called a "wise passiveness." Here is how Simone Weil describes the state of mind necessary if we are to really pay attention:

> Attention consists of suspending our thought, leaving it detached, empty, and ready to be penetrated by the object. . . . Above all our thought should be empty, waiting, not seeking anything, but ready to receive in its naked truth the object that is to penetrate it. (111–12)

Of course, complete emptiness is almost unimaginable and perhaps humanly impossible, but Weil's description applies to diverse religious reading and meditative traditions that teach practices for uncluttering the mind, calming the body.

. . . as flawed human beings we always see "through a glass, darkly."

To learn more about traditional practices of scriptural reading, I interviewed Mary Westfall, the minister of our community church and frequent chaplain at university services. I realize that biblical reading is not, and often cannot, be any part of school instruction. There are useful boundaries between church and state, between schools and organized religion. Yet for centuries this was the primary reading anyone did; it was intense, consequential, repeated, meaningful reading, and was built on the belief that this text was never fully understood, never comprehended, that as flawed humans we always see "through a glass, darkly." It is the most essential, profound, long-standing form of slow reading I can cite.

In my conversation with Reverend Westfall, I was struck by the parallels to the case I am making and made aware that the roots of these reading practices in long-standing traditions of biblical reading. For example, she mentioned the concept of *Midrash*, a rabbinical practice of exploring a text:

> The Hebrew rabbis do a lot of Midrash. You see the letters on the page—that's the black fire. The white space around it—that's the

white fire. When you are reading your eyes are taking in the black fire but what is not there, the empty spaces, are as much part of the story as the letters themselves. And so I try to invite people to think about the white fire; those empty spaces are a mystery but they are also what we bring to the text.

One rabbi extended this comparison, claiming that the letters, the black fire, represented the stable, foundational, intellectual component of the message.

The white spaces, on the other hand, represent that which goes beyond the world of the intellect. The black letters are limited, limiting and fixed. The white spaces catapult us into the realm of the limitless and the ever-changing, ever-growing. They are the story, the song, the silence. Sometimes I wonder which speaks more powerfully, the black, rationalistic letters or the white, mystical spaces between them. (Weis)

This is a distinction that a reader of any age can understand.

Reverend Westfall described several practices that allow the reader to fill in the white space, to create the white fire of reading:

- **WORK WITH SMALL UNITS.** There can often be an ambition to read the whole Bible, which can be daunting and even defeating after a while. It is more productive to explore in depth much smaller units (a single verse or parable).

- **ADOPT A TRUSTING ATTITUDE.** A starting point for reading is "a trusting attitude, a belief that there is something that can emerge from the reading that is not apparent in the first quick read." It is the trusting that texts can never be exhausted or consumed, never known once and for all—that they continue to speak, console, provoke, counsel. "It's the confidence that you'll leave with more than you came in with. People are amazed and say, 'That was all there?' Well it was in the interaction." Implicit in this stance is the valuing of *repeated readings* (something children know but adults forget).

- **ENTERING A STATE OF MINDFULNESS.** The reader needs "to enter into a slowed down space, meditative space, a thoughtful space—and so to be actually present to something." Unlike Weil, Reverend

Westfall does not claim to be "emptied," because we always read through "the particularities of our life experience," but the preparatory time, beginning with silence and an attention to breathing, can bring the reader to a state of receptiveness where we can be attentive. We cannot entirely eliminate these preoccupations, but we can become aware of them, and there are rituals that can help us set them aside momentarily, so we can concentrate and achieve the "intentionality to be present."

- **ATTEND TO WORD MEANINGS.** One of the techniques Westfall uses is for readers to jot down words that seem strange, engaging, puzzling. "On a slower reading some word will jump out at you— Why do they say '*Fear of God is the beginning of wisdom*'? What does *fear* make you think of? If you have study resources, you can learn that the Hebrew word means 'awe and wonder'—and that's a very different meaning." She also encourages her readers to pay attention to "irksome" passages—in one case, a member of her study group resisted a story from Acts where people who were telling a lie just dropped dead. "That's hard for twentieth-century minds, so the question is: What is that bringing up for you? And it's bringing up all the issues of how unrealistic things happening in the Bible are. So I ask, 'What if it's metaphoric? What might that be meaning? Does it mean 'shrivel inside'? So she becomes an exegete herself."

  One strategy that she uses to attend to words is to form her study group in a circle and to have the group read the passage, one word per person, and then have people pull out action verbs or words that convey emotion. This activity places scrutiny on each word.

- **READ WITH THE FULL BODY.** Mary spoke of prompts used in Bible study groups that invite readers to engage all of the senses—"It will ask questions about what you smell, taste, hear as you read the test. It's amazing just how reading something will trigger a memory, and when the passage talks about a certain thing—we smell it, bread baking, we smell the perfume. It's interesting that reading can be such a full-bodied experience." It is particularly important that these texts, drawn from oral traditions, be heard; different voices with different intonations can open new meanings. "It is important to remember that that scripture was first dripping off someone's lips before it became solid on the page.

There is a more organic sense to the spoken word that people feel. Instead of just a cerebral experience, it becomes cellular."

- **THE SERMONIC EYE.** The question that drew me to this interview in the first place was the process of elaboration that allows a minister to build an entire sermon around a single verse or set of verses (a pericope). I will quote Mary at length on this question:

> I have out my "sermonic eye." I'm always trying to see "How does this shed light on . . . ?" "How does it relate to this situation?" "What is the engagement between that text and human experience?" And if I have the text in my head in advance, it's amazing the things the world throws at you. I've often thought of the T. S. Eliot quote: "We have the experience but we miss the meaning." The great thing about being a clergyperson is that we know that every experience is dripping with meaning—and is a possible sermon. . . .
>
> I approach scripture as one way to tell the human story—and so every day that story keeps being retold. In one sense, I love reading scripture. But on the other hand, it can be useless if one saw it as "This is the rule to live by." From my perspective, it is the unfolding story about why we are here. What is this life about? How do we live knowing we are going to die? Is there something we can count on? We are continually trying to create and reflect on this story of human experience. And week after week, month after month, season after season, human strengths and foibles appear everywhere.

My father was not religious in any conventional sense, never a church-goer. He would recite a short prayer before dinner, "Be present at our table, Lord. Amen." But that seemed to be the extent of his interaction with any god. He seemed to me a thoroughgoing materialist. Yet near the end of his life, hobbled by strokes, he became a regular Bible reader. His Bible was used and worn, the spine broken and held together by a rubber band. The pages were marked up and annotated in his unique, laborious, architectural handwriting (we suspect he was naturally left-handed and converted to right-handed penmanship in elementary school). His markings were similar to the way he marked other books: he had the habit of placing a box around some word on every page, and whenever I read one of his books, I would lose concentration trying to figure out his system (I never did figure it out).

In these last few months, he would read aloud each day, the Forty-sixth Psalm, which began:

> God is our refuge and strength, a very present help in trouble.
> Therefore will not we fear, though the earth be removed,
> and though the mountains be carried into the midst of the sea.

In his eighty-sixth year, he broke his hip and failed to recover, losing weight until his face was so thin his false teeth no longer fit. On a December afternoon, the day after an arduous trip from Ohio to a senior living facility in Maine, he began to decline. My brother, a physician who was with him at the time, describes the last couple of hours, consoling him with the music of his daughter-in-law, with the poetry of his best friend, and, as his "earth was removed," with his favorite Bible passage—a reader to the end. Here is his description:

> On his final day, he was clearly fading. I suggested that we take him to the hospital. He couldn't speak, but his eyes conveyed that he wanted to stay where he was. So after a moment, I came back to his room, told him that we weren't going anywhere and that I would sit with him. I must have read the psalm twenty times over the next hour or two until he died. We listened to a recording of Cheryl's playing the Ravel Piano Concerto, second movement. I can barely listen to that now. I read some of Dick's poetry. But the last thing was the psalm.
>
> I've always felt this psalm hinges on the line: "Be still and know that I am God." Toward the end, I emphasized the "Be still" words. And, in time, he was.

WHY CAN'T THEY BE LIKE WE
WERE, PERFECT IN EVERY WAY?

It isn't funny anymore. The Dumbest Generation cares little about history books, civic principles, foreign affairs, comparative religions, and serious media and art, and it knows less. Careening through their formative years, they don't catch the knowledge bug, and tradition *might as well be a foreign word.*

—MARK BAUERLEIN, *THE DUMBEST GENERATION*

As I write, Stieg Larsson's Girl with the Dragon Tattoo trilogy remains firmly atop the *New York Times* best-seller list, where it has been for months. The Swedish version of the films have made their way across the country, and there has been a buzz about the casting for the English version. The "girl" is, of course, Lisbeth Salander, abused as a child, hunted down by a corrupt old guard with unlimited resources and unwarranted confidence that their secrets are secure. To combat them, Lisbeth has personal toughness and a dazzling ability to use the computer, to hack and penetrate, to communicate with Mikael and with other hackers, who have taken up her case. And she brings her tormentors down.

Equally, as I write, Tahrir Square in Cairo is the scene of celebratory demonstrations after the fall of Hosni Mubarak, dictatorial ruler of Egypt for thirty years. Like Lisbeth's persecutors, he had all the conventional advantages: a security apparatus of police, informers, and torturers; control of television and newspapers; "emergency" powers that he retained for almost all of his reign. He even had his hands on the switch of the Internet that he shut off when demonstrations started. But he was met with physical courage *and* a superior knowledge of technology. Demonstrators found ways to make phone calls that converted into Twitter messages; they communicated with TV reporters from El Jazeera and CNN and helped expose the police brutality in suppressing demonstrations; they made laughable Mubarak's claim that outsiders were responsible. And they brought him down in seventeen days. In the afterglow of the protests, many of the leaders effusively praised Mark Zuckerberg, the twenty-six-year-old creator of Facebook. Here is what Wael Ghonim, an Egyptian employee of Google and symbol of the revolution, said in an interview after Mubarak's downfall:

> I want to meet Mark Zuckerberg one day and thank him . . . I'm
> talking on behalf of Egypt. . . . This revolution started online.
> This revolution started on Facebook. This revolution started . . .
> in June 2010 when hundreds of thousands of Egyptians started
> collaborating content. We would post a video on Facebook that
> would be shared by 60,000 people on their walls within a few
> hours. I've always said that if you want to liberate a society just
> give them the Internet. (LaCapria)

We need to keep Lisbeth and the Tahrir demonstrators in mind when any of my generation feels the urge to denigrate students today for their use of media. I'm thinking of the title of Mark Bauerlein's recent book, *The Dumbest Generation: How the Digital Age Stupefies Young Americans and Jeopardizes Our Future (Or, Don't Trust Anyone Under 30)*. This hits all the hot buttons—media is making our children and students "dumb," and this dumbness is threatening "our" future. It inverts the slogan of our college years about not trusting anyone *over* thirty. The book itself is not quite as strident as the title, but it reflects a tired, and I believe unfounded, generational narrative of decline. (As an aside, I feel my own generation—which has accumulated a huge national debt, has fought dubious wars without paying for them, and has failed to ensure entitlement programs for our children—could more easily qualify as "the dumbest"—though that's an assertion for another time.)

Steven Johnson has pointed out in a very different book, *Everything Bad Is Good for You*, intelligence tests continually have to be renormed upward; the one hundred–point average has risen from the time my generation took these tests, a change that Johnson attributes to the demands of a more complex media environment. A movie like *The Matrix* would have been incomprehensible to an earlier generation raised on TV shows like *Gunsmoke* and *The Andy Griffith Show*. The secretaries in *Mad Men*, with their Selectric typewriters, seem to occupy a numbingly simple world.

Even for those who don't buy Johnson's claim (and Bauerlein clearly doesn't), the statistics I've seen show no decline in reading ability (no great gain either). The National Assessment of Academic Progress shows a virtual flat line from 1992 to the present. I have seen no precipitous decline in the preparation of my own students. I am old enough to have had the parents of my current students in class. And I work on the same things—elaboration, complexity, focus, close reading. It's fair to say that our students read about as well, or as poorly, as their parents—but they also have technological, accessing, and social networking skills that are not tested—and that an older generation continually scrambles to master. What teacher has not been stumped by some form of media, often something mysterious like an "on" switch, and pleaded to students, "Can any of you help me out with this?" More often than not, someone from this dumbest generation comes forward to assist us.

As I see it, there are two stances adults can take that earn the justified scorn of a younger generation. One is to dismiss out of hand the media interests and skills of this new generation, to compare them unfavorably with more established traditions, to fail to see any value in them, to view them as less thoughtful, less cognitively demanding, antisocial, or, to use Bauerlein's term, as *stupefying*. Invariably, these judgments are made by adults who have not engaged this media themselves—as James Gee once said to me, "The people who criticize *Grand Theft Auto* couldn't get the car out of the garage." I regularly hear the claim that video games destroy concentration and I want to ask, "Really, have you ever seen someone play?" Our first move should be ethnographic—that is, to take the stance that forms of media use "makes sense" in some way: There is some gratification, some challenge, some meaning involved. Humans don't voluntarily persist in activity they find meaningless.

This is not to argue that distraction, immoderation, even addiction are not problems. I have students who, thinking that they have a text message, can't restrain themselves from checking their phones—it doesn't matter

The secretaries in Mad Men, with their Selectric typewriters, seem to occupy a numbingly simple world.

where they are. But distraction is not a new problem. The addictive personality will find some outlet, some attachment for that addiction—though we tend to think more highly of older attachments (card playing, even reading) than newer ones like video games and using social networks. Paying attention has *always* been difficult, which is why religious and meditative traditions have such elaborate means of focusing. Anyone who has a tendency toward depression knows the feeling of a mind racing, reviewing past failures, as if it has its own means of propulsion and direction. The challenge of being fully present, of being *there*, of being in control of our own thinking, is one that the ancients wrote about; it is perennial.

I believe we can also lose credibility by failing to stand up for traditions that matter to us, some that we build within families and schools, some that we carry forward from previous generations. Even children who rebel must rebel against something, and great innovations in art and music have been made by those who knew and appreciated the traditions they were rebelling against. In this book, I have tried to make a case for older practices of reading slowly and deliberately—of attending to words, to sounds, to the "irksomeness" of some texts. I have called on support for this position from a cast of thinkers stretching two millennia, and I did this not to appear academic but to be grounded, to place myself in traditions that I value.

Even as students explore the possibilities of new media—as they develop expertise in multimodal composing and "reading"—they will need traditional skills. As Deborah Brandt has wisely argued in her book *Literacy in American Lives*, the social change rarely involves the wholesale discarding of older skills; rather, the process is additive. The student who creates a digital story must learn new skills involving the integration of music, narration, visuals; she must explore visual means of transition. But she also must *tell a story*, using detail, dialogue; she must create characters, conflict—skills as old as storytelling itself. How many contemporary movies fail because they try to substitute special effects for good writing and storytelling?

Not all of these practices I advocate here will help students with the testing that is so determinative these days. One teacher told the story of a very deliberate student who would sabotage herself on tests by patiently working through the decoding of nonsense words that she couldn't immediately identify; "On these tests, honey, just skip it," the teacher wisely counseled.

But I believe these slower practices can give readers power. For if we allow ourselves a slower pace, time for rereading and reflection, we can take on harder things. As we adopt a "growth mind-set," we can embrace difficulty and not view it as a personal shortcoming. Whether these practices will improve our standing in international economic competition, whether they will help us make up ground on Finnish children, I can't say. And frankly, I don't care.

Ultimately, we need a good reason to ask students to read in an age with so much competition for attention. There may be a few students out there who can get excited by the rallying cry of "rigor." There are surely some who feel gratified by good test scores. There may even be some far-sighted ones who can get excited by the argument for going head-to-head with the Chinese. But these strike me as weak arguments, extrinsic arguments. The case I make in this book is that we read for pleasure and meaning—and to do so, we must be able to control the tempo of our reading. And that by slowing down, by refusing to see reading as a form of consumption or efficient productivity, we can attend to word meanings and sound, building a bridge to the oral traditions that writing arose out of. We can hold passages in memory, we can come to the view that good texts are inexhaustible, to the belief that the white spaces always invite us to reflect and expand.

Reading instruction should make this slowness possible. We need to put away the stopwatches and say in every way possible—"This is not a race. Take your time. Pay attention. Touch the words and tell me how they touch you."

WORKS CITED

Allard, Harry, and James Marshall. 1981. The Stupids Die. New York: Houghton Mifflin.

Applebee, Arthur. 1978. *The Child's Concept of Story*. Chicago: University of Chicago Press.

Atwell, Nancie. 2007. *The Reading Zone: How to Help Kids Become Skilled, Passionate, Habitual, Critical Readers*. New York: Scholastic.

Austen, Jane. 2011. *Pride and Prejudice*. New York: Tribeca.

Ballou, Sullivan. 1861. "Sullivan Ballou Letter." Available at www.pbs.org/civilwar/war/ballou_letter.html.

Bartholomae, David. 1983. "Writing Assignments: Where Writing Begins." In *Forum: Essays on Theory and Practice in the Teaching of Writing*, edited by Patricia Stock. Upper Montclair, NJ: Boynton/Cook.

Bartholomae, David, and Anthony Petrosky, eds. 2002. *Ways of Reading: An Anthology for Writers*, 6th ed. Boston: Bedford/St. Martin's.

Bauerlein, Mark. 2008. "Online Literacy Is a Lesser Kind." *The Chronicle of Higher Education* (September 19). Available at http://chronicle.com/article/Online-Literacy-Is-a-Lesser/28307.

———. 2009. *The Dumbest Generation: How the Digital Age Stupefies Young Americans and Jeopardizes Our Future (Or, Don't Trust Anyone Under 30)*. New York: Penguin.

Baxter, Charles. 1999. "Introduction." *Ploughshares* (Fall). Available at www.pshares.org/read/article-detail.cfm?intArticleID=4695.

Bergson, Henri. 1976. *An Introduction to Metaphysics: The Creative Mind*. Towata, NJ: Littlefield, Adams.

Bernays, Anne, and Pamela Painter. 2009. *What If? Exercises for Fiction Writers*, 3d ed. Upper Saddle, NJ: Longman.

Bernstein, Jeremy. 1981. "Profiles: Marvin Minsky." *The New Yorker* (December 14): 50–128.

Berry, Wendell. 1994. "An Entrance to the Woods." In *The Art of the Personal Essay*, edited by Phillip Lopate. New York: Anchor Books.

Berthoff, Ann. 1981. *The Making of Meaning*. Portsmouth, NH: Boynton/Cook.

Bianchi, Lisa. 1999. "Finding a Voice: Poetry and Performance with First Graders." PhD diss., University of New Hampshire.

Birkerts, Sven. 1994. *The Gutenberg Elegies: The Fate of Reading in an Electronic Age.* New York: Fawcett Columbine.

Bizzell, Patricia, and Bruce Herzberg, eds. 2001. *The Rhetorical Tradition: Readings from Classical Times to the Present.* Boston: Bedford.

Brandt, Deborah. 2001. *Literacy in American Lives.* Cambridge: Cambridge University Press.

Britton, James. 1971. *Language and Learning.* Miami: University of Miami Press.

Brooks, David. 2007. "The Outsourced Brain." *New York Times* (October 26). Available at www.nytimes.com/2007/10/26/opinion/26brooks.html.

Brower, Reuben. 1962. "Reading in Slow Motion." In *In Defense of Reading,* edited by Ruben A. Brower and Richard Poirier, 3–21. New York: Dutton.

Brown, Claude. 1965. *Manchild in the Promised Land.* New York: Macmillan.

Buckley, Christopher. 2011. "Dad at a Distance": A Review of *My Father's Fortune* by Michael Frayn. *New York Times Book Review* (March 6): 1, 10.

Burke, Kenneth. 1931. *Counter-Statement.* Berkeley: University of California Press.

Callahan, Raymond. 1962. *Education and the Cult of Efficiency: A Study of the Social Forces That Have Shaped the Administration of the Public Schools.* Chicago: University of Chicago Press.

Carr, Jean Ferguson, Stephen Carr, and Lucille Schultz. 2005. *Archives of Instruction: Nineteenth-Century Rhetorics, Readers, and Composition Books in the United States.* Carbondale: Southern Illinois University Press.

Carr, Nicholas. 2008. "Is Google Making Us Stupid?" *Atlantic Monthly* (July/August). Available at www.theatlantic.com/doc/print/200807/google.

———. 2010. *The Shallows: What the Internet Is Doing to Our Brains.* New York: Norton.

Channing, Edward. 1823–1851. List of Subjects for Student Themes. Cambridge, MA: Harvard University Archives.

Chekhov, Anton. 2003. "The Darling." In *Ward No. 6 and Other Stories,* edited by David Plante, translated by Constance Garnett, 247–60. New York: Barnes and Noble Classics.

Cisneros, Sandra. 1991. *The House on Mango Street.* New York: Vintage.

Cole, Luella. 1938. *The Improvement in Reading with Special Reference to Remedial Instruction.* New York: Farrar and Rinehart.

Coleridge, Samuel Taylor. 1839. *Aids to Reflection*. New York: Stanford and Swords.

Collins, Billy. 2005. "The Trouble with Poetry." In *The Trouble with Poetry: And Other Poems*. New York: Random House.

Connors, Robert J. 2003. "The Erasure of the Sentence." In *Selected Essays of Robert J. Connors*, edited by Lisa Ede and Andrea A. Lunsford, 452–78. Boston: Bedford.

Crews, Donald. 1996. *Shortcut*. New York: Greenwillow.

Crews, Harry. 1998. "The Car." In *Life Studies: An Analytic Reader*, 6th ed., edited by David Cavitch, 366–70. Boston: Bedford.

Cunningham, Michael. 2010. "Found in Translation." *New York Times* (October 3): WK 10.

Dahl, Roald. 1998. *Fantastic Mr. Fox*. New York: Puffin.

Daly, Jill Eileen. 1997. "Simply Chris." In *Fresh Ink*, Vol. 1, 23–27. Boston: Boston College.

Dawson, Rebecca. n.d. "The Writing Mentor Project: An Invitation to Readers." In *English 501 Handbook*, edited by Thomas Newkirk. Durham: University of New Hampshire.

"Dear First Lady Michelle." 2010. *New York Times* (November 27): WK 10.

Dewey, John. 1910. *How We Think*. Boston: D. C. Heath.

Dickens, Charles. 1953. *The Life and Adventures of Nicholas Nickelby*. Oxford, UK: Oxford University Press.

Dickinson, Emily. n.d. "A Narrow Fellow in the Grass." Available at www.online-literature.com/dickinson/824/.

Didion, Joan. 1978. "Interviews: Joan Didion, The Art of Fiction." *The Paris Review* 71 (Fall/Winter). Available at www.theparisreview.org/interviews/3439/the-art-of-fiction-no-71-joan-didion.

Dransfield, J. Edgar, with William McCall. 1925. "Technique for Teaching Silent Reading." *Teachers College Record* 26 (9) (November): 740–52.

Drew, Christopher. 2011. "Rethinking AP." *New York Times* (January 9): 24–27 (Education Life).

Dweck, Carol S. 2010. "Even Geniuses Work Hard." *Educational Leadership* 6 (1) (September): 16–21.

Elbow, Peter. 2000. "The Shifting Relationships Between Speech and Writing." In *Everyone Can Write: Essays Toward a Hopeful Theory of Writing and Teaching Writing*. New York: Oxford University Press.

————. 2011. *Vernacular Eloquence: What Speech Can Bring to Writing*. New York: Oxford University Press.

Erasmus. 2001. *The Adages of Erasmus*. Toronto: University of Toronto Press.

————. 2007. *On Copia of Words and Ideas*. Translated by Donald B. King and H. David K. Rix. Milwaukee: Marquette University Press.

Fitzgerald, F. Scott. 1925. *The Great Gatsby*. New York: Scribners.

Flower, Linda. 1981. *Problem-Solving Strategies for Writing*. New York: Harcourt, Brace, Jovanovich.

Franzen, Jonathan. 2001. *The Corrections*. New York: Farrar, Straus, and Giroux.

Gallagher, Kelly. 2010. "Reversing Readicide." *Educational Leadership* 67 (3) (March): 36–41.

Gantos, Jack. 2002. *Hole in My Life*. New York: Farrar, Straus, and Giroux.

Gardner, Howard. 2002. "Test for Aptitude, Not for Speed." *New York Times* (July 18). Available at www.nytimes.com/2002/07/18/opinion/test-for-aptitude-not-for-speed.html.

Geertz, Clifford. 1977. "Deep Play: Notes on a Balinese Cockfight." In *The Interpretation of Culture*, 412–54. Boston: Basic Books.

————. 1983. *Local Knowledge: Further Essays in Interpretive Anthropology*. New York: Basic Books.

Getzels, Jacob W., and Mihaly Csikszentmihalyi. 1976. *The Creative Vision: A Longitudinal Study of Problem-finding in Art*. New York: John Wiley.

Gilb, Dagoberto. "Victoria." In *The Best American Essays: 1999*, edited by Edward Hoagland. Boston: Houghton Mifflin.

Gladwell, Malcolm. 2005. *Blink: The Power of Thinking Without Thinking*. Boston: Little, Brown.

Good, James. I. 1901. *Aid to the Heidelberg Catechism*. Cleveland: Central Publishing Company.

Gorlick, Adam. 2009. "Media Multitaskers Pay Mental Price, Stanford Study Shows." *Stanford Report* (August 24). Available at news.stanford.edu/news/2009/august24/multitask-research-study-082409.html.

Gould, Stephen. 1981. *The Mismeasure of Man*. New York: Norton.

Graff, Gerald, and Kathy Birkenstein. 2006. *They Say/I Say: The Moves That Matter in Academic Writing*. New York: Norton.

Groopman, Jerome. 2007. *How Doctors Think*. New York: Houghton Mifflin.

Harvard University Library. 2010. "Interrogating Texts: 6 Reading Habits to Develop in Your First Year at Harvard." Available at http://hcl.harvard.edu/research/guides/lamont_handouts/interrogatingtexts.html.

Harvey, Stephanie, and Harvey Daniels. 2009. *Comprehension and Collaboration: Inquiry Circles in Action*. Portsmouth, NH: Heinemann.

Heaney, Seamus. 1980. "Death of a Naturalist." *Poems 1965–1975*. New York: Farrar, Straus, and Giroux.

Hedin, Robert. 1982. "Tornado." *Poetry* 140: 28.

Honore, Carl. 2004. *In Praise of Slowness: Challenging the Cult of Speed*. New York: HarperCollins.

Huey, Edmund Burke. 1921. *The Psychology and Pedagogy of Reading*. New York: Macmillan.

Jobs, Steve. 2005. Stanford commencement speech. Available at http://news.stanford.edu/news/2005/june15/jobs-061505.html.

Johnson, Steven. 2006. *Everything Bad Is Good for You: How Today's Popular Culture Is Actually Making Us Smarter*. New York: Penguin.

———. 2010. "Yes, People Still Read But Now It's Social." *New York Times* (June 20): BU 3.

Johnston, Peter. 2004. *Choice Words: How Our Language Affects Children's Learning*. Portland, ME: Stenhouse.

Joyce, James. 1916/1967. "The Dead." In *The Experience of Literature*, edited by Lionel Trilling, 624–51. New York: Holt, Rinehart, and Winston.

———. 1956. *A Portrait of the Artist as a Young Man*. New York: Penguin.

Kamen, Leslie P., and Martin E. P. Seligman. 1987. "Explanatory Style and Health." *Current Psychological Research and Reviews* 6 (3) (Fall): 207–18.

Karelitz, Ellen. 1993. *The Author's Chair and Beyond*. Portsmouth, NH: Heinemann.

Katz, Amanda. 2010. "Former English Major Who's 'Not Good at Reading.'" (October 10). Available at www.boston.com/ae/books/articles/2010/10/10/former_english_major_whos_not_good_at_reading/.

Keats, John. 1817. "Letter to George and Tom Keats." Available at www.litencyc.com/php/stopics.php?rec=true&UID=%20766.

Keene, Ellin. 2008. *To Understand: New Horizons in Reading Comprehension*. Portsmouth, NH: Heinemann.

Keene, Ellin, and Susan Zimmermann. 2007. *Mosaic of Thought: The Power of Comprehension Strategy Instruction*, 2d ed. Portsmouth, NH: Heinemann.

Kennedy, John F. 1961. John F. Kennedy inaugural speech draft. Available at www
.ourdocuments.gov/doc.php?flash=true&doc=91#.

Kenyon, Jane. 1990. *Let Evening Come*. St. Paul, MN: Greywolf Press.

Kerr, Michelle. 2010. "ACT Reading Speed Is Faster Than SAT to Obtain a High
Score." Available at http://collegepuzzle.stanford.edu/?m=201012.

King, Martin Luther Jr. 1964/1988. "Letter from a Birmingham Jail." In *The Borzoi
Reader*, 6th ed., edited by Charles Muscatine and Marlene Griffith, 650–66.
New York: Knopf.

LaCapria, Kim. 2011. "Freed Google Executive Ghonim Thanks Facebook
for Role in Egyptian Revolution." Available at www.inquisitr.com/98197/
wael-ghonim-thanks-facebook/.

Lee, Harper. 1960. *To Kill a Mockingbird*. New York: Lippincott.

Lewis, Norman. 1944. *How to Read Better and Faster*. New York: Thomas Y.
Crowell.

Lindberg, Gary. 1986. "Coming to Words: Writing as Process and the Reading of
Literature." In *Only Connect: Uniting Reading and Writing*, edited by Thomas
Newkirk, 143–57. Upper Montclair, NJ: Boynton/Cook.

Lunsford, Andrea A., John Ruszkiewicz, and Keith Walters. 2007. *Everything's an
Argument with Readings*, 4th ed. Boston: Bedford.

Luria, Alexander. 1987. *The Mind of a Mnemonist: A Little Book About Vast
Memory*. Cambridge, MA: Harvard University Press.

Manguel, Alberto. 1996. *A History of Reading*. New York: Viking.

McCourt, Frank. 1999. *Angela's Ashes*. New York: Scribners.

McGuffey's Fifth Eclectic Reader. 1879. Cincinnati: Van Antwerp, Bragg, and Co.

Miedema, John. 2009. *Slow Reading*. Duluth: Litwin.

Mitchell, Joseph. 2008. *Up in the Old Hotel*. New York: Vintage.

Modern Times. 1936/2010. Special ed. DVD. Directed by Charles Chaplin. New
York: Criterion Collection.

Moffett, James. 1983. *Teaching the Universe of Discourse*. Boston: Houghton
Mifflin.

Moje, Elizabeth Birr, et al. 2008. "The Complex World of Adolescent Literacy."
Harvard Educational Review 78 (1): 107–54.

Monroe, Lewis. 1871. *Monroe's Fifth Reader*. Philadelphia: Copperthwait and Co.

Moss, Ann. 1996. *Printed Common-Place Books and the Structuring of
Renaissance Thought*. Oxford, UK: Clarendon.

Mumford, Lewis. 1934. *Technics and Civilization*. New York: Harcourt Brace.

Murray, Donald. 1980/2009. "Writing as Process: How Writing Finds Its Own Meaning." In *The Essential Don Murray: Lessons from America's Greatest Writing Teacher,* edited by Thomas Newkirk and Lisa Miller, 6–26. Portsmouth, NH: Boynton/Cook.

———. 1982. "Teaching the Other Self: The Writer's First Reader." *College Composition and Communication* 33: 140–47.

Muske-Dukes, Carol. 2002. "A Lost Eloquence." *New York Times* (December 29). Available at www.nytimes.com/2002/12/29/opinion/a-lost-eloquence.html.

Nabokov, Vladimir. 1955. *Lolita.* New York: Putman's.

National Assessment of Educational Process. 2009. *Grade 12 Reading and Mathematics. The Nation's Report Card.* Washington, DC: National Center for Educational Statistics. Available at http://nces.ed.gov/nationsreportcard/pdf/main2009/2011455.pdf.

New Zealand National Film Unit. 1989. *I Can Read* (videocassette). Portsmouth, NH: Heinemann.

Newkirk, Thomas. 1982. "Young Writers as Critical Readers." *Language Arts* (May): 451–57. http://www.eric.ed.gov/ERICWebPortal/search/detailmini.jsp?_nfpb=true&_&ERICExtSearch_SearchValue_0=EJ264225&ERICExtSearch_SearchType_0=no&accno=EJ264225

———. 2009. "Stress, Control, and the Deprofessionalizing of Teaching." *Education Week* 29 (October 21): 24–25.

———. 2010. "The Case for Slow Reading." *Educational Leadership* 67 (March): 6–11.

Noyes, Alfred. n.d. "The Highwayman." Available at www.potw.org/archive/potw85.html.

O'Brien, John. 1922. *Silent Reading: With Special Reference to Methods for Developing Speed. A Study in the Pedagogy and Psychology of Teaching.* New York: MacMillan.

Ong, Walter. 1975. "The Writer's Audience Is Always a Fiction." *PMLA* 90 (January): 9–21.

Opie, Iona, and Peter Opie. 1959. *The Lore and Language of Schoolchildren.* London: Oxford University Press.

Orwell, George. 1952/1995. "Such, Such Were the Joys." In *The Art of the Personal Essay*, edited by Phillip Lopate. New York: Anchor Books.

Palgrave, Francis. 1861. *The Golden Treasury.* London: Macmillan.

Percy, Walker. 1975. "The Loss of the Creature." In *The Message in the Bottle*, 46–63. New York: Farrar, Straus, and Giroux.

Plato. 2001. "The Phaedrus." In *The Rhetorical Tradition: Readings from Classical Times to the Present,* edited by Patricia Bizzell and Bruce Herzberg. Boston: Bedford.

Plutarch. 1941. *The Lives of Noble Greeks and Romans.* Translated by Thomas North. New York: Heritage Press.

Poirier, Richard. 1997. "Reading Pragmatically." In *Pragmatism: A Reader,* edited by Louis Menand, 403–55. New York: Vintage.

Polanyi, Michael. 1958. *Personal Knowledge: Toward a Post-Critical Philosophy.* Chicago: University of Chicago Press.

Pollan, Michael. 2008. *In Defense of Food: An Eater's Manifesto.* New York: Penguin.

Postman, Neil. 1979. *Teaching as a Conserving Activity.* New York: Delta Books.

———. 1985. *Amusing Ourselves to Death: Public Discourse in the Age of Show Business.* New York: Penguin.

Prose, Francine. 2006. *Reading Like a Writer.* New York: HarperCollins.

Quintilian. 1990. "From *Institutes of Oratory.*" In *The Rhetorical Tradition: Readings from Classical Times to the Present,* edited by Patricia Bizzell and Bruce Herzberg. Boston: Bedford.

Rasinski, Timothy, and Pamela Hamman. 2010. "Fluency: Why It Is 'Not Hot.'" *Reading Today* (August/September): 26.

Reilly, Mary. 2009. "Dressing the Corpse: Professional Development and the Play of Singularities." *Journal of Curriculum and Pedagogy* 6 (1) (Fall): 79–99.

Roethke, Theodore. 1962. "Moss-Gathering." In *Words in the Wind.* Bloomington: Indiana University Press.

Roosevelt, Franklin. 1945. "Draft No. 1. Proposed Message to Congress." Available at www.archives.gov/education/lessons/day-of-infamy/images/infamy-address-1.gif.

Rose, Mike. 1989. *Lives on the Boundary.* New York: Penguin.

Rosenblatt, Louise. 1980. "What Facts Does This Poem Teach You?" www.eric .ed.gov/ERICWebPortal/search/detailmini.jsp?_nfpb=true&_&ERICExtSearch_ SearchValue_0=EJ229985&ERICExtSearch_SearchType_0=no&accno= EJ229985*Language Arts* 57 (4) (April): 386–94.

———. 1994. *The Reader, the Text, and the Poem: The Transactional Theory of the Literary Work.* Carbondale: Southern Illinois University Press.

Rosenthal, Nadine. 1995. *Speaking of Reading.* Portsmouth, NH: Heinemann.

Saenger, Paul. 1997. *Space Between Words: The Origins of Silent Reading*. Stanford, CA: Stanford University Press.

Salinger, J. D. 1951. *Catcher in the Rye*. New York: Little, Brown.

Scieszka, Jon. 2008. *Knucklehead*. New York: Viking.

Seneca. 1932. "On the Shortness of Life." Loeb Classical Library. Translated by John W. Basore. London: Heinemann. Available at http://forumromanum.org/literature/seneca_younger/brev_e.html.

———. 1969. *Letters from a Stoic*. New York: Penguin.

Service, Robert. n.d. "The Cremation of Sam Magee." http://wordinfo.info/unit/2640?letter=C&spage=26

Shakespeare, William. 1948. *Antony and Cleopatra*. In *Shakespeare: The Complete Works*, edited by G. B. Harrison. New York: Harcourt, Brace, and World.

Shirky, Clay. 2008. "Why Abundance Is Good: A Reply to Nick Carr." *Encyclopedia Britannica Blog*. Available at www.britannica.com/blogs/2008/07/why-abundance-is-good-a-reply-to-nick-carr.

Simic, Charles. 1994. "Poetry Is the Present." In *The Unemployed Fortune-Teller: Essays and Memoirs*, 53–57. Ann Arbor: University of Michigan Press.

"Sleep and the Raveled Sleeve of Care." Available at http://aheadofthewave.blogspot.com/2009/01/sleep-and-raveled-sleeve-of-care.html.

Smith, Frank. 1983. *Essays into Literacy: Selected Papers and Some Afterthoughts*. Portsmouth, NH: Heinemann.

Sommers, Nancy, and Laura Saltz. 2004. "The Novice as Expert: Writing the Freshman Year." *College Composition and Communication* 56 (1): 124–49.

Sorby, Angela. 2005. *Schoolroom Poets: Childhood, Performance, and the Place of American Poetry*. Lebanon, NH: University Press of New England.

Spinelli, Jerry. 1990. *Maniac Magee*. New York: HarperCollins.

Sterne, Laurence. 1965. *The Life and Opinions of Tristram Shandy, Gentleman*. Boston: Houghton Mifflin.

Thoreau, Henry David. 2000. *Walden and Civil Disobedience*. New York: Houghton Mifflin.

Thorndike, Edward. 1921. "Measurement in Education." *Teachers College Record* 22 (5) (November): 371–79.

Trelease, Jim. 1982. *The Read-Aloud Handbook*. New York: Penguin.

Trillin, Calvin. 1984. "The Best Restaurants in the World." In *The Contemporary Essay*, edited by Donald Hall. Boston: Bedford/St. Martin's.

Trimble, John. 1975. *Writing with Style: Conversations on the Art of Writing.* Englewood Cliffs, NJ: Prentice-Hall.

Twain, Mark. 2001. *The Adventure of Tom Sawyer.* New York: Modern Library.

Virgin Mobile. 2010. *Terms of Service: payLo.*

Vonnegut, Kurt, Jr. 1969. *Slaughterhouse-Five or The Children's Crusade: A Duty-Dance with Death.* New York: Dell.

Vygotsky, L. S. 1978. *Mind and Society: The Development of Higher Psychological Processes.* Cambridge, MA: Harvard University Press.

Weil, Simone. 1992. *Waiting for God.* New York: Harper.

Weis, Avi (Rabbi). "A Taste of Torah in Honor of Shabbat." Available at www.hir.org/a_weekly_gallery/8.16.02-weekly.html.

Weizman, Ilana, Eva Blank, and Rosanne Green. 2000. *Jokelopedia: The Biggest, Best, Silliest, Dumbest Joke Book Ever.* New York: Workman.

Whitehead, Alfred North. 1967. *The Aims of Education and Other Essays.* New York: Free Press.

Whitman, Walt. 1955. *Leaves of Grass.* New York: Signet.

Willingham, Daniel T. 2009. *Why Students Don't Like School.* San Francisco: Jossey-Bass.

Wolf, Maryanne. 2007. *Proust and Squid: The Story and Science of the Reading Brain.* New York: Harper.

INDEX